MORE
UNSOLVED
MURDERS

MORE UNSOLVED MURDERS

JIM MORRIS

AMBERLEY

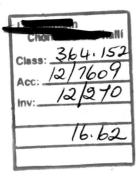
First published 2012

Amberley Publishing
The Hill, Stroud
Gloucestershire, GL5 4EP

www.amberley-books.com

British Library Cataloguing in Publication Data.
A catalogue record for this book is available from the British Library.

ISBN 978 1 4456 0689 7

Typeset in 10pt on 12pt Sabon.
Typesetting and Origination by Amberley Publishing.
Printed in the UK.

CONTENTS

INTRODUCTION

Finding out the number of crimes, particularly murder, which go unsolved in the UK each year is not an easy task, and a couple of the cases here would give more than one person a sigh of relief if they had been solved. When police services are asked about the number of unsolved murders or cold cases they have, some blatantly refuse to give any figures and those that do may not give entirely reliable responses. For instance, a lady was strangled in 1967 and a gentleman was later acquitted, so he wasn't guilty: an unsolved crime, but it isn't on record as such. It gives Mr and Mrs Joe Public a far better sense of comfort to hear about the crimes that have been solved, rather than the ones that haven't.

Generally speaking, most murders are domestic affairs where a wife, husband or partner is no longer desired or required, and there might be a tidy sum to pick up on the life insurance. Such cases leap out at the police and an arrest is soon made. Other people have volatile relationships and not everyone can control their emotions; this is not to say anyone who is overcome by anger is likely to kill, but it does raise the possibility. When faced with such strong emotions, most of us can compose ourselves with a sit-down and a cup of tea; however, some people can't do this and the anger turns into a rage that can escalate into all sorts of violent and illegal actions.

It is not pleasant to think that we might be living next door to a murderer, even when the evidence is clear. Mr So-and-so's wife has gone missing but everyone thinks she has simply left him, we don't want to consider that she is actually buried somewhere in a shallow grave. Then there is the murder in furtherance of other crimes and, whether we like it or not, to some crime can be a career. But there are people who kill for other, quite unknown reasons. This is evil and one can only hope for a solution.

Finally, though this is intended to be an illustrative rather than exhaustive summary, there are a group of people who may experience an escalation of emotion, which leads to an explosion somehow, somewhere for the most innocuous of reasons. And, although the clues are there, it is not always an easy job to identify the killer and bring them to justice.

This book is another selection of fascinating unsolved murder cases where the clues didn't lead the police anywhere. However, I do include and discuss one conviction and a hanging – as an execution abolitionist, this is the entire crux of the book. And it might be better to have no conviction at all than convict the wrong man. The other four cases show how closely the police might move towards the culprit, but then they might also be on the wrong track.

In the case of the conviction resulting in hanging, the murdered woman was seen by a significant number of people after the time of death given by the pathologist, when the man convicted with the crime had an alibi. For a couple of people to make a mistake and say they saw someone on a Saturday when it was really a Friday is possible, but for around ten people to see someone on a certain date doesn't stretch credibility, it breaks it. It is well worth considering this crime in detail.

The Second World War took men overseas and many would write a letter home to show that all was well; similarly, the women would write to their husbands, provided they weren't murdered in the oddest of places – such as a disused bus garage.

Marriages end for a number of reasons and murder is sadly one of them, but what happens when the body is never found and the husband dies of a heart attack shortly after the event? Where can the police take the inquiry? Are they justified in closing the case and not looking for another suspect?

The pleasant couple of old-time dancers and their two sons lived in happy domesticity until the wife is bludgeoned to death. There was not even a whiff of a motive, so how can the police get on the killer's trail?

Can a suspect be brought to trial when he can neither hear nor answer the charge against him? Would it come down to the judge telling the jury that they could not possibly decide guilt or innocence of a deaf mute's supposed confession? A seventy-eight-year-old retired school teacher is bludgeoned to death, but by whom?

This book highlights five more murder cases; four where there was nowhere for the inquiry to go, and one that quite legitimately could go somewhere – like back to the Court of Appeal.

ACKNOWLEDGEMENTS

My sincere thanks are due to a number of people, some of whom might think their contribution was small, but it was nevertheless essential.

The staff of The National Archives at Kew and The British Library at Colindale are almost a national asset in how hard they work for people like me, and they do it so cheerfully too.

Stockphotography has thousands of photographs, almost a picture for all occasions. Adam Bruderer is a solo photographer who is consistently helpful.

Claire MacDonald whose images really are a superb addition to any text.

I have a considerable debt to Sarah Flight and Jonathan Reeve at Amberley Books, whose perseverance should be the subject of a book in itself. Also Tom Furby at Amberley, his help has been both gracious and patient.

Finally, thanks to Kelly Owen's editorial assistance; this book is the richer for her input.

MARY COMINS, SCARBOROUGH, 1943

The Silver Grid pub in Huntriss Row in Scarborough was certainly a pub with history. One former mayor was quoted to have said that he would cross the road to avoid the place, and it was not finally tamed until a retired professional boxer became licensee in the late 1960s/early 1970s.

It was on a Sunday night in 1943 that Mary and Edna met Dick and Jimmy. It was not known who was in the pub first, but they had arranged to meet at 7.00 p.m. Dick and Jimmy were soldiers; Dick was a corporal and Jimmy a private. The four of them left to visit another pub, the Hole in the Wall, sometime later, but at some point in the later evening – Edna said it was around 10.00 p.m. – the four of them split into two couples: Jimmy with Edna and Dick with Mary. Edna said she eventually parted from Jimmy in Westborough in the town centre at around 10.45 p.m. and started to make her way home. She lived in Wrea Lane, which was about a twenty-minute walk. As she got close to home, in Dean Road from which Wrea Lane turns off, she actually saw Mary again. This was at about 11.00 p.m. and Mary was with another man who Edna later said was 'I believe, a soldier. He certainly wasn't a civilian.' Mary crossed the road to Edna and they discussed the two soldiers they had been with earlier; Mary said of their proximity to home, 'I'll be down in a few minutes Eddie.' At that time, Edna thought Mary was perfectly alright.

Edna could not tell for sure if the man was in uniform or not, or what service the uniform was for – in the blackout with no street lights this is not surprising. As it was later confirmed that both Dick and Jimmy had (separately) returned to their base by taxi, and the man Edna saw Mary with at 11.00 p.m. was not wearing an overcoat as Dick was, it made his identification next to impossible. And he stood in the shadows. But it was this man that Mary almost certainly went to a disused bus garage with, and it was here that she was strangled on the night of Sunday 21 March 1943. She was thirty-three years of age. Her body was dumped face down in about 2 ½ inches of water and oil in an inspection pit in the garage. One of the first things the police later wished to establish was whether Mary went to this garage willingly with this man and, if so, for what reason. Although there were some superficial bruising on Mary's body there was no evidence of 'interference'.

Mary Elizabeth Taylor had married Jack Comins in her hometown of Middlesbrough in December 1935; he was three years younger – there were no children. Mary was a brown-eyed blond, described as very attractive and of a pleasant character. Edna said she and Mary had been friends for many years and spent a great deal of time in each other's company. Edna was feeling the loneliness of young mums in the war; she had a daughter of four years and her husband was away in Scotland with the Royal Artillery.

Jack Comins was away in North Africa, Tunisia, at the time of his wife's death. He was in the Military Police attached to the 8th Army under General Montgomery. From 19 March, the 8th Army were involved in a battle south-east of the Matmata Hills at the Mareth Line – about 250 miles south of Tunis and 1,500 miles south-east of Scarborough. Things were sort of going the 8th Army's way, but the 15th Panzer Division launched a counterattack on 22 March. General Horrocks took an armoured division around the west side of the Matmata Hills and emerged through the Tobago Gap to the north of the enemy forces. With General Montgomery to the south, General Horrocks to the north and flanked by the Matmata Hills to the west and the Mediterranean Sea to the east, the enemy were running out of options. So, in the latter part of March, Jack Comins had a fairly busy time and, of course, a sound alibi.

Mary and Edna came down from Middlesbrough to Scarborough as eighteen-year-olds for seasonal work at the Astoria Hotel, and Mary met Jack, who was a local lad. She had worked in a hotel up to a year before, but was employed at the time of her death at a grocer's shop in Prospect Road. Mary and Jack actually had Edna and her husband, Joe, to stay with them for about a year after they married.

On the Monday morning, Edna went to Jordan's grocers, where Mary worked, to shop, but found her friend was not at work. She then called on another friend who was related to Mary, and by the evening their level of worry was sufficient to prompt them to contact the police. The report was noted but at that stage the police could do nothing. Mary's brother was reported to have searched Mary's home in the hope of finding some clue as to what was going on, but he discovered nothing. Mary's neighbours said they had not seen her since the Sunday morning but they said she was out more often than not.

The disused bus depot in Vine Street where Mary's body was found had only recently been vacated and had been 'used by the Military'. In her statement to the police, Edna mentioned the garage and The Green Howards in the same sentence (this regiment had a long association with Yorkshire and they were active in the Second World War – in fact the only VC awarded on D-Day went to Company Sergeant-Major Stanley Hollis of The Green Howards). In March 1943, the sergeants were billeted at the Rivelyn

Hotel so there was some presence. This made the job of investigating the murder far more difficult. In particular, to eliminate suspects the police had to go to extraordinary lengths to track people down to interview. One can imagine that if the garage was only vacated the day before the murder then the police would want to follow this lead up as a high priority. Did someone know their way around this building and how it was secured when the 'Military' left?

In the event, the garage had not been properly secured and local children got in to play. One of them, Thomas Johnson, had seen the body on the Monday 22 March but when he told his mother she dismissed it as being a 'dummy' so the matter rested for a day or two. Thomas lived in Trafalgar Road West but had friends who lived at the eastern end of the bus garage in Vine Street. It was on the Wednesday 24 March that Thomas had dared to venture into the garage again where he met his friend, Irene Mayes. Irene knew the body was not a dummy and so went to find an older boy to help. Her next-door neighbour, Bobby Wood, was sixteen, and it was Bobby who went to the police. As it was clear a murder inquiry would ensue, the Chief Constable wasted no time in calling in the assistance of Scotland Yard.

It is difficult for writers, as well as readers, to imagine wartime. The war, by 1943, was such a fixture in life that it may have been a case of 'live today'? Mary's social life was scrutinised, and when interviewing Edna the police could not shy away from the subject of Mary's private life. Edna said:

Mrs Comins had no children and I know that since her husband joined the Army, she has been very friendly with numerous soldiers, who have either been on a visit to or stationed at, Scarborough. She knew heaps and heaps of soldiers and I am quite sure she must have had affairs with some of them, although she has never given me any facts. She has never told me that she had 'fallen' for any particular soldier, with the exception of a Sergeant in the Air Force ... and I know that whenever he could get away from his wife he would come to Scarborough and meet her. He used to sometimes spend the night with some people ... She would see him there and sometimes spend the night there.

One hopes he survived the war. Edna added, 'She gave soldiers the impression that she was a woman of loose morals, but I am under the impression that she would lead them on, but no more. She had that way with her.' On the Wednesday, when Irene Mayes and Bobby Wood had gone to the police, a Sergeant Halford had gone back to the garage in Vine Street with them. Sgt Halford realised at once that the situation would warrant further police investigation, so he sent a junior colleague to summon the police surgeon and the local CID.

Dr Noel Herbert attended the crime scene at around 6.00 p.m. on the Wednesday evening (24 March). Dr Herbert concluded that a 'slight struggle' had taken place but could only find superficial bruising on Mary's body. The scene was photographed before Mary's body was removed to the mortuary pending a post-mortem examination.

Professor Peter Sutherland from Leeds University performed the post-mortem on 26 March. He could confirm death was due to strangulation, probably manual (the assailant's hands) but was unable to give a definitive time of death.

The scene of the crime was noted to have some marks where it was thought likely the crime occurred and then the body was dragged across the yard before it was dumped in the inspection pit. This suggested that the crime took place in the garage, and Prof. Sutherland thought the murder had been committed by just the one person. There were no reports of any damage or tears in Mary's clothing, which was consistent with her entering the garage voluntarily rather than being forced. There were reports of screams that night, but the witnesses who heard were a long way off, though it was discovered that the garage gave a good echo. If Edna had waited at the junction of Wrea Lane and Dean Road, it is more than possible she would have heard the screams – therefore there is some doubt. The lower half of Mary's dress and coat had risen up but this was probably because of her being dragged, feet first, across the garage to the pit. So this reinforced the theory of where the crime took place. This led to the question of what Mary was doing in the garage.

When Edna had seen her late on the Sunday night, about an hour after the two couples had parted, she was in Dean Road, opposite the end of Wrea Lane where both women lived. Edna later said in the Coroner's Court:

> I called over to Mary, and she came across the road and asked if the gentleman I had been with had 'missed the truck' and I said 'Yes. He had gone to catch a taxi.' That is all. She left me there, saying that she would see me in a few minutes …

But Edna had said a little more in her police statement, or at any rate gave a little more detail: Mary had said to her that 'the man she had been with had also gone to get a taxi.' Therefore, the man Mary was with at this later time was someone she had met after she and Dick had parted company.

So the scene was that the two, Mary and Edna, had met Dick and Jimmy by prior arrangement in a pub, they later went to a second pub before parting company. There is no mention of any further pub visits, so the inevitable question is, what was the activity of each couple between around 10.00 p.m., when they parted, and 11.00 p.m. when they saw each other close to home? One can only guess, but would people easily equate this with the normal routine of wives at home, or was it slightly out of the ordinary?

From the point at which Edna later saw and spoke to Mary, Dean Road goes north-west, and the junction with Trafalgar Street West is only about 150 yards or so. In Trafalgar Street West was an entrance to the bus garage.

Hole in the Wall pub in Scarborough. It was here that Mary and Edna parted. But where did Mary go before she got to the Bus Garage? (Copyright Adam Bruderer)

There was a fairly extensive investigation led by Detective Chief Inspector Arthur Thorpe of Scotland Yard. Dick and Jimmy were traced and eliminated from the inquiry. There was the usual mention of anonymous information coming in, 'suggesting particular lines of enquiry'. It was reported some of the anonymous information was traced to serving soldiers – not the most likely group one would expect to hide behind anonymity, unless with reason. All the lines of inquiry were followed up with the CID in Scarborough and the Scotland Yard officers (DCI Thorpe had DS Albert Griffin with him) travelling far and wide to interview mobilized military units. One problem the police encountered was the mobility of the military at this point in the war – the unit Dick and Jimmy were in could well have been moved south (which is probable). So the police had a lot of background work tracing people before they could further their investigation. This made for a prolonged and time-consuming investigation.

On 8 May 1943, Mr Claude Royle, the coroner, recorded a verdict of 'Murder by person or persons unknown'. Media reports at the time encouraged the public to try and help, and appeals for witnesses continued. But one wonders the impact on the public of statements in the press such as, 'She was seen a good deal in the company of men friends in uniform, with who she not infrequently visited licensed premises.' And, 'As already stated deceased was seen a great deal in licensed premises and elsewhere in the company of soldiers.'

Madam Judgement and her wagging tongue would almost certainly have led some folk to make their own conclusions, and it is difficult to consider this case and avoid making assumptions. It was wartime and one wonders just how many folk thought, 'To hell with it there is a war on – live today!' And it was as simple and as innocent as that – one individual picked up the wrong message from Mary, and her fate was sealed.

Just how many people who could have given the police information but were reluctant to do so less the police thought they too were part of this 'social scene' is unknown. This case does remind one of the age-old problem of the inherent dangers of the 'world's oldest profession'. But it may have been far more straightforward, though equally as dangerous, if Mary was 'leading them on'. As Edna said, 'I am under the impression that she would lead them on, but no more.'

The names Dick and Jimmy were taken from newspaper reports at the time. The official file, or the majority of it, is exempt from the Freedom of Information Act, and just as well. Therefore, my guess is that the names are pseudonyms. I hope they survived the war.

Edna died in the 1990s.

The killer of Mary Comins was never found.

Portrait of Mary Comins.

LINDA STURLEY, BIGGIN HILL, 1982

It has to be said that averages often conceal a truth. A random sample of deaths in Kent in 1982 revealed the average age was seventy-five years and nine months – give or take a day or two – but this conceals the fact that one of the deceased was ninety-seven years of age and, sadly, more than one was below one year. The 'second youngest' was fifty-seven years and so on, but it is two individuals departing from this 'norm' that I want to discuss: Graham Sturley was thirty-seven when he died, and his wife, Linda, was probably twenty-nine. I say 'probably twenty-nine' because her body was never found, and so she was almost certainly murdered.

It can be an uphill struggle to prove murder without a body but not an impossibility, and several cases of murder have resulted in conviction without a body, notably Messrs Hossein for the murder of Mrs Muriel McKay in the late 1960s/early 1970s, and more recently the case in Swindon of Glyn Razzell convicted for the murder of his wife, but this is open to question.

Graham Sturley met Linda Hollands when he was trying to scrape a living as a taxi driver. The two hit it off almost at once, and reports suggest a detour, or at any rate a stop along the way for Graham's taxi that night.

He had a number of jobs during his remarkable-yet-short career: private detective, shopkeeper and what was loosely described as a property developer at the time of his death. When he was a shopkeeper he was apparently selling stolen goods so was 'away' for about a year. On his return to the rat race he found work driving a taxi and met Linda.

The couple married and settled into domestic bliss in Biggin Hill, Kent. But almost at once Graham took a lover, and so did Linda. Things soon began to go awry; there were frequent rows where sometimes blows would be exchanged. But despite this, Graham was on good terms with Linda's side of the family, and their marriage produced two children.

Graham had tried to 'investigate' her behaviour by 'tapping' the 'phone – he actually discovered her making plans to meet someone, and when he confronted her with this

Portrait of Linda and her (estranged) husband, Graham.

they reconciled their relationship. But the reconciliation did not last for long, and apparently the presence of the children did not inhibit either Graham or Linda.

Linda worked as a representative for the Avon Cosmetics company. She was from a fairly close family, and this is something I will return to, but it was Linda's sister who had last seen her on 17 July 1981 when she had visited. Linda told her that Graham had beaten her and punched her in the stomach during a violent argument the night before, when he raged that one of her lovers was the father of the child she was expecting.

Linda was, at this point, six months pregnant.

On the morning of 18 July 1981, Linda's sister called around to see her, but was told by Graham that Linda had gone away. He was on good terms with Linda's family and they had no reason to doubt him.

But it is at this point that the mystery starts to deepen. Not simply the mystery of Linda's disappearance, but how her family dealt with it. She was said to be close to her mother and sisters, so why was it over a year before her disappearance was brought to the attention of the police?

Mrs Ada Webb, Linda's mother, went to the police and persuaded them to investigate. Clearly, the stories Graham had given for her continued absence had ceased to be plausible. But if he had repeatedly assured the family Linda was safe and well, then how did he get around Christmas and birthdays? If Linda had really only 'gone away' then would her absence at birthdays and Christmas not have aroused suspicion? Even the absent parent would send gifts to their children, and most girls in their late twenties or more mature years would not miss their mum's birthday.

Graham had actually told his children of their mother's departure and for that year until July 1982, he lived as if Linda had simply gone away. He had forged her signature to take everything out of her savings accounts and he cashed the cheques for her maternity benefit payments.

It was at around 7.00 a.m. on 17 August 1982 that the police arrived at the 'marital home' and asked Graham where on earth Linda was.

He told them, 'Yes, she's gone and I don't expect to see her again. I don't know where she is and I'm glad to get rid of her.' He openly admitted to them his hatred for her flaunted love affairs with other men.

The police questioned him closely, but the investigation was to take a heavy toll on him. He had not been well for years with a heart condition and was on medication. He also smoked cigarettes, and his consumption grew. He told police:

I believe that Linda is alive, I feel that she is alive. I have got so much hate within me for her, but in no way would I want to see her dead. I suppose that, wherever she is, unless she is a very long way away, she must know what is going on, and so the reason that she has not come forward must be spite.

On the night she left, he said they had 'a normal, average sort of row' in which he slapped her across the face and cut her lip, but he denied punching her in the stomach.

'I was very, very pleased when I found she had gone in the morning. She had slept on the living room settee that night; she often did, so I never heard her go.'

He found the police questioning frightening. At one stage during a staggered session, which lasted over fifteen hours, one of the police officers asked him, 'Why don't you tell us? We know you did it.'

Graham said, 'They were direct, very direct. It wasn't very nice, but what the hell can you do?'

But he did have a lot of explaining to do, and there can be no doubt that he had the know-how, the motive and the opportunity to have murdered her.

It was Detective Chief Superintendent Algernon Hemingway who led the hunt for Linda Sturley. He and his colleagues were at a terrible disadvantage because Linda had been missing for well over twelve months. But, slowly, the detectives began to piece together the facts.

Linda Sturley's family doctor described the pregnancy and revealed that she would need to give birth to her baby by a Caesarean section. This is an operation that needs a high level of medical and nursing input and is accompanied by hospitalisation for a number of days, if not longer. Records were checked for every hospital in the country but no one of Linda's description had been admitted. No birth was subsequently registered, and the cost of the operation would not have been met in other countries without recourse to the National Health Service. In short, the baby could not possibly have been born without a record somewhere.

Intense publicity in national newspapers and on television and radio failed to bring any sign of Linda. Her family had also told detectives that Linda was very attached to her children and Linda would never voluntarily leave them.

So the search began for her body.

The police were quoted to have said, 'We know your wife had a string of lovers and she was a bad wife. And we understand that sometimes pressure like that can drive a man to murder.' But Graham never faltered once during long sessions of police interrogation, even at one stage taunting them with 'You'll have to prove it.' He quipped that 'You think I have buried her in the garden. Well I wouldn't have been so silly, that would have poisoned the flowers.'

It was only a matter of time, the police thought, before they found Linda's body and broke through his angry defiance to gain a confession.

'She had walked out on me so many times in the past I didn't bother to report her as a missing person. I'm glad she's gone, I never want to see her again.'

The floorboards were lifted in the living room of the house and brickwork probed for hidden cavities. Infrared and heat-seeking detection equipment was used to scan the gardens around the house and tracker teams with dogs combed the surrounding woodland and parks. Police divers searched lakes, streams and ponds, and forensic experts were sent to examine the bones of a woman's body unearthed in a forest thirty miles away. But there was no sign of Linda, dead or alive, and moreover no evidence that her body had been dismembered in the house.

Graham's neighbours claimed he had a bonfire and burned her clothes, but when the police searched the house they found her clothes in the wardrobe. Linda's jewellery was in her jewellery box. But would he leave her clothes as she had left them? On a more practical note, Graham moved his new partner in, so where did she hang her clothes?

However, all of this is a sidetrack.

After three months of intensive investigation, DCI George Cressy examined all the circumstantial evidence and decided he had enough to recommend arresting Graham for the murder of his wife. However, Graham Sturley died of a heart attack, and the murder inquiry on Linda Sturley was closed, the case file marked 'Suspect deceased'. His solicitor disposed of his assets and said, 'A will was left by Mr Sturley disposing of his assets, but there was nothing dramatic in it one way or another, no confessions, no admissions.'

The detectives did not attend the funeral, but someone knew something! There was a cryptic message on a wreath: 'Well you got that out of the way, Sturley. All my love.'

Officially, it is an unsolved murder. Two points though. Firstly, what if he had not murdered her? The police had, what they felt, was a good circumstantial case against him, and there are times when circumstantial evidence is more potent than, say, eyewitness evidence. And there was more, and it would be worth thinking for a moment about the disposal of Linda's body.

After Graham's death, the police were still tying up the loose ends and one detective made a call to his house. There was no one in, but Graham's car was on the drive and when he tried the handle the officer found the car was unlocked. Of course it had been searched earlier but this detective seemed to have his eyes open.

He found a map under the front seat, and in true 'whodunit' style there was an 'X' marked. But this was not as flippant as I suggest – the officer considered what the 'X' indicated, it was a farm. So the officer drove to the location: a huge pig farm that was just a few miles away outside Farnborough in Kent. With the owner's permission, the farm was searched by 100 soldiers and police officers. And they made the grim discovery of a woman's shoes and toes.

The farmer had been out on the night of 17 July– the day Linda disappeared – and had not returned until early the next morning. Graham had attempted to rent a cottage close to the farm a few months before. There was a strong argument that he had killed her there and brought the body to the farm where it was thought he had cut the body into pieces, and fed portions to the pigs.

Nothing official was ever released by the police of this, and there would certainly have been forensic follow-up to it.

No (other) remains of Linda Sturley were ever found.

PENELOPE MOGANO, COVENTRY, 1954

Carlo Mogano was of Italian parentage but was born on the Isle of Wight in 1908. He married Penelope Norris in 1931; she was a year younger. They left the Isle of Wight and moved to Coventry where they settled and had two sons. Mrs Mogano was a full-time housewife and mother; Mr Mogano was a production manager at the Daimler factory. They moved into their house in Holland Road, Radford, just six years after the end of the war. Their previous house had been damaged by the bombing and, for a time, Mrs Mogano and the two sons had returned to her hometown of Ryde on the Isle of Wight. After the war, things settled, and there was a large amount of repair work undertaken in the city, including the magnificent Coventry Cathedral.

It was at around 1.45 p.m. on Monday 18 January 1954 that Mrs Mogano's husband returned to work after having lunch at home. Their younger son also finished his lunch at that time and headed back to Bablake School. Mrs Mogano was to visit friends that afternoon, but this never happened. The youngest son found the house locked when he returned home from school at 4.50 p.m. He would have been home sooner but had called in at the laundrette to collect a bundle of laundry for his mum. When he got home he found both the front and back door locked, so waited for his father.

When Mr Mogano returned from work he let himself and his son into the house. It was in the dining room that he found his wife slumped in an armchair, next to the television. There was heavy blood-staining on the walls, and it was clear that a lot of force had been used to kill her. There were many head wounds and medical examination revealed that her face and tongue had been slashed with a carving knife; a twelve-inch carving knife was found next to her body. However, the house had not been touched insofar as robbery was not an apparent motive.

Mr Edward Pendleton, Chief Constable of Coventry City Police, said, 'It was a particularly vicious murder ... she received many head wounds.' He did not hesitate to call in Scotland Yard.

It was soon reported to the police that a 'bogus inspector' from the Electricity Board had been knocking on doors in Mrs Mogano's neighbourhood to discuss any problems with television reception.

Coventry Police were quick to follow this up. They issued a description of the man: 'a black-haired young man with a slight London accent ... and he wore a dirty khaki dust-coat.' He apparently made '... suggestions of an indecent nature ... (and in) the past week similar complaints have been made...'

At least five incidents had been reported in the week previous to Monday 18 January, and the man visited a house within 150 yards of Mrs Mogano's home. His methods were said to be that he would check the meters, but once inside the house his behaviour would become less decorous.

A further police statement said:

> The following described man is wanted for interview: Aged 25 to 30, height 5ft. 2in. to 5ft. 6in., thick and possibly wavy black hair, full face and fresh complexion. He is dressed in a dark blue overcoat, similar to uniform coat, believed shiny buttons, red plaid shirt with collar attached, no tie, no hat.

The Coventry City Police worked initially to piece together the recent past of Mrs Mogano. One area of inquiry was the couple's enthusiasm for old-time dancing, which had an active social side. Mrs Mogano was to visit friends that afternoon – Mr Sydney Worrell and his wife. Mr Worrell himself was the victim of a strange attack a few days before when an attempt was made to set fire to his pantry, but the police treated this as a separate incident. A couple of months before, on bonfire night, someone ignited petrol-soaked rags in a car on Mr and Mrs Mogano's driveway, but they dismissed this as a prank.

Throughout the night of Monday 18 January, the police saw many of the Moganos' friends from the old-time dancing circle. House-to-house enquiries were also commenced: 'Did you see Mrs. Mogano, or any person visiting her between 1.45 and 5.45 pm yesterday'.

In keeping with usual police practice, the last person to see Mrs Mogano alive was interviewed at length. And he happened to have been the person who discovered the body. Mr Mogano finally left the police station at five o'clock the next morning after an approximate ten-hour interview. The focus of the interview was the old-time dancing circles they moved in. A team of officers interviewed all members of the dancing club at their 'base', the Savoy Ballroom.

Although a carving knife had been found next to Mrs Mogano, there was another weapon used – possibly a hammer. As soon as light allowed, the search began for this. The Radford area was thoroughly searched: particular gardens, Radford Common and all ponds. The house was searched for clues.

Professor James Webster was called to do the post-mortem. He reported that Mrs Mogano was battered to death, and sustained several blows to the head, probably with a hammer; likely a round-headed hammer. Otherwise Mrs Mogano had been quite healthy. There was no evidence of recent sexual activity. Prof. Webster was able to fix her time of death at between 3.00 and 4.00 p.m.

With such an assault, the murderer would have been extensively splashed and would have had blood, tissue and possibly skull fragments on his clothing. But the police did not immediately discount the possibility that the assailant could have been female. They formed the theory that the assailant knocked at Mrs Mogano's door between around 3.00 and 4.00 p.m. and was invited in. This suggests either it was someone she knew or it was the plausible story of the 'electricity meter man'. After the attack, the front and back door of the house were locked.

Detective Superintendent John Edmunds and Detective Sergeant Ted Williams arrived from Scotland Yard. They read through the statements collected thus far; but little was known. In Holland Road, where Mr and Mrs Mogano lived, they were known as a quiet couple, whose main interests were their garden and their old-time dancing.

As Mrs Mogano was friendly with Mr and Mrs Worrell from their old-time dancing circle and she was to visit them that afternoon, the police took statements from them. They also re-examined reports from colleagues who had investigated following the report of fire in their pantry only two nights before the murder. Mr Worrell was a leading figure in the old-time dancing group, which led the police to think there might be someone with a warped grudge against some members of the group. This would be difficult to follow up, as to all outward appearances their behaviour would be acceptable but they would lose all rationale if thinking about the target of their hatred.

DSupt Edmunds examined the police photographs of the murdered woman and the layout of the room in which the body was found. Later, with his colleague, he went to the house and reconstructed the scene in the dining room where Mrs Mogano had been found.

The theory of a grudge was quite well supported, particularly in view of what was now at hand but also with the 'wad of rag soaked in lighter fuel ... put under the bonnet of a car in the Mogano's drive and ignited'. It was thought the person responsible did not know it was not Mr Mogano's car. And then there was the strange incident with the attempted arson at their friend, Mr Worrell's house.

House-to-house checks in the district continued, and a twelve-man team of detectives were taking statements. Drains in the district were searched for the other weapon, which was probably a hammer.

On the 'suspect' front, the search for the 'black-haired young man with the slight London accent' was stepped up as the reports of instances where he had tried to gain access to houses were now over twenty in the week of the murder. On each occasion, access to the house resulted in 'improper suggestions'. His last reported 'call' was at around 1.30 p.m. on the afternoon Mrs Mogano was murdered, and it was only about 150 yards away. A man answering the description was seen in a local pub, and he was seen by another witness 'lurking' by some bushes outside the pub. There was also a sighting near the Savoy Ballroom, which was the meeting venue of the old-time dancing group Mr and Mrs Mogano belonged to.

However, a window cleaner who was in Holland Road at the time of the attack did not see anyone who he thought resembled the man.

Detailed medical examination told the police that Mrs Mogano's killer struck with fanatical frenzy. There were at least twelve hammer and knife wounds on her head. The police thought Mrs Mogano may have picked up the carving knife to try and defend herself and that it was snatched from her grasp and used by the killer.

Hammers in the house were examined but none were similar to the one believed to have been used in the attack.

And then the police got a bit of a breakthrough. A married lady of twenty-five was at home, less than a mile away from the scene of the crime with her two young children. The 'electricity meter man' called at her house. She later described him:

> The most noticeable thing about him was the red plaid shirt, open at the neck. Otherwise, apart from his thick, curly hair and rosy complexion, he was a man you wouldn't particularly notice. He had a nice musical laugh and seemed younger than 25.

Apparently the man busied himself first by testing the switches so there was a real possibility that a full set of fingerprints were left. The lady added, 'He handled the 'point' for some time, and ... no one else has touched it .... While he talked to me, he told me his home town, but I have been so flustered by all the trouble that it has gone from my mind ... it is a London suburb ...'

He was in her house for about fifteen minutes, and was initially polite and cheerful. She went on to say:

> I told him to come in and pointed out that the meter was in the pantry. He followed me through the living room into the kitchen, and as I turned round he was close up behind me. He laughed and pointed to a switch on the wall saying, 'I want to see those switches. We are having lots of interference with TV sets around here and you should get suppressors on these.' For a few minutes he messed around with it and then came back into the middle of the room and stood with his hands on the table. He just stared at me, and it was then I began to realise something was wrong ... he stared so long it became embarrassing.

He became chatty again but;

> he asked me who lived in the house and asked (son) where his daddy was and if
> he came home to dinner. It was just after this that his conversation took a different
> course and eventually I told him to go ... he went out, gave a final look through the
> front window and made off at a fast pace towards the railway station at Coundon.

DSupt Edmunds requested a fingerprint expert from Scotland Yard. Fingerprints had
been taken from Mr and Mrs Mogano's dining room but unfortunately there was no
match on record.

Mr Mogano had his own view of the investigation and he told the press that he
wanted to be very clear that his view was that they had no enemies in the old-time
dancing club and he did not think any one of the people they had known would have
been responsible for Mrs Mogano's death:

> We were just one happy family at the Dancing Club. There were no secrets between,
> my wife and myself, and she had no particular dancing partner other than me. As far
> as I know she hadn't an enemy in the world. I think it was impossible that she knew
> her attacker.

But the 'electricity meter man' was never far from the centre of the inquiry and there
was a theory that someone was shielding him. Reports were still coming into the police
about his activities, as far away as London and more locally in Birmingham. Lorry
drivers were under scrutiny and the police prioritised efforts to talk to café proprietors.
There was talk of a lorry and the police described a vague inquiry they were following
up: a 'green-painted lorry' with the name 'Cooper' on the side. It was seen in the
Midlands area before the day of the murder, so the police wished to talk to the driver
to ask if he could recollect giving anyone a lift. House-to-house inquiries continued in
what was described as an ever-widening circle in the city.

A heavily bloodstained handkerchief was found near a city centre building site, but
this did not lead anywhere.

The inquest opened but was soon adjourned. Evidence was taken from Mr Mogano
who explained that his wife was forty-four, and the last time he saw her alive was at
lunchtime on Monday. He returned home at 5.40 p.m.

'She was reclining in a chair and obviously dead,' he said.

Prof. Webster reported that from his post-mortem examination:

> Obviously she had very grave injuries. She was fully clothed ... she had injuries of
> three types. The total number of injuries ... was more than 25. The first type were
> defensive or protective injuries ... to her hands which she had obviously held up to

protect herself. She had cuts or wounds made by an instrument such as a knife ... in the main to her mouth, severing not merely the lips, but almost cutting the tongue in two. The third group of injuries were the more serious. They were inflicted by a blunt instrument, such as a hammer. So great was the damage she had no floor to the base of the skull. This had caused considerable damage to the brain and she was almost bled white. This ... had been a healthy woman.

He said the cause of death was shock from multiple injuries, which included gross fracture of the skull and lacerations to the brain.

And yet more reports came in of the 'electricity meter man' – said to be operating in Birmingham. Twelve more police officers were transferred to the inquiry to make a total of seventy engaged in the hunt, and this number was expected to grow. Bloodstains were found on a 'phone book in a 'phone box outside a post office just around the corner from Mr and Mrs Mogano's home; however, police were not optimistic about finding a link.

A questionnaire was distributed to homes in Radford, though this was later extended. Initially 1,500 questionnaires were completed. Police wanted to know the name of the person, age, height, any regular callers to their home and their reasons for calling, their usual pattern of calling, occasional callers and when – particularly on 18 January. Further, did they know Mrs Mogano, did they see her on 18 January, and did they see her talking to anyone? Any unusual or unknown vehicles (cars were far fewer than today). Old time dancing and other 'guild' activities were also enquired after. But although this did bring in new information, any arrest was still a long way off.

But DSupt Edmunds said that a fingerprint had been discovered at Mr and Mrs Mogano's home, which, he said, was 'an important one'. Chief Constable Mr Pendleton was sure that some tiny detail which might seem insignificant could well take the inquiry forward. He said, 'Wherever you were on January 18 go over the day minute by minute and no matter how insignificant a detail may seem please get in touch...'

Meanwhile, hundreds of completed questionnaires were being scrutinised and some 'very interesting details' emerged. But there were still gaps in the known activities of Mrs Mogano, particularly in the afternoons. And no information was forthcoming on anyone in Holland Road between the hours of 2.00 and 5.00 p.m. on Monday 18 January. The area the questionnaire was distributed in was again extended.

During a press conference, the police said they were 'convinced' that someone was withholding information, and this may have been because of affection, fear or because they themselves were involved. There were still gaps in what the police knew of Mrs Mogano's routine, and they were anxious to speak to anyone who had seen her in the previous few weeks. Detectives visited cafés, pubs and even spoke to bus conductors. A man who answered the description of the 'electricity meter man' was detained. A spokesman said:

> A man accompanied local detectives and Scotland Yard officers to the Central Police Station in connection with the complaints from various householders in Coventry about his gaining entrance on the pretence of TV interference and examining electric meters. These inquiries followed on police inquiries into the murder of Mrs Penelope Mogano.
>
> The man was stopped on the by-pass in a blue lorry bearing the name 'Cooper.' There was another man in the vehicle. It is understood that he ... gave an address near London. He was still at the Central Police Station as inquiries were made into his movements over the past few weeks ...

This lead fizzled out though. But soon the police were active again. It was thought the killer had grappled the carving knife from Mrs Mogano, who had picked it up to try and defend herself. So when a witness reported seeing a man leave a telephone kiosk on the day of the murder with his right hand wrapped in a makeshift bandage – probably a tea towel – the police wished to follow this up. The lady who reported this believed she could identify the man.

Mr Pendleton said, 'We would ... like to interview anyone who saw this man in the telephone kiosk and any person who knows of a man who received a cut hand on Monday. January 18.'

The police issued a description and this differed from the 'electricity meter man' but the lady said she had a good look at him and would be able to recognise him again. She looked through five volumes of police photographs but could not identify the man, it was planned that she should view similar photographs in Birmingham and possibly even Scotland Yard. Another witness also came forward to make what was described as 'an important statement'. The police then repeated their appeals for information; it was now nearly two weeks since the murder.

The 'phone box was subjected to rigorous investigation and parts of it were even taken to the forensic laboratory for testing. The telephone directory in the kiosk was noted to be bloodstained. Unfortunately it was a common blood group so did not really help. A few weeks before, a Coventry City Police detective had been injured in an incident where he was 'stabbed seven times' in this kiosk. The wounds were to his arm though and the blood found in the kiosk matched his blood.

A major lead came in with the discovery of a bloodstained handkerchief that bore the initials 'P. R.' in black ink. It was a plain white handkerchief found in Crampers Field, which was in the Radford area, and police thought it might prove the vital link in the inquiry. Mr Pendleton appealed for witnesses: 'We would like the owner of this handkerchief or anyone who knows the owner to contact us immediately.'

Portrait of Penelope Mogano.

'Holland Road in the Radford area as it is in 2011. A nice, friendly neighbourhood. But in 1954 a monster lurked.'

Laundries were visited but police activity was limited without more information. However, the police made enquiries with chemists and doctors for anyone approaching for treatment or dressings for cuts.

Mr Pendleton added, 'We would like anyone who knows of a person who was injured on January 18 to contact us.' Police eventually traced the owner of the handkerchief marked 'P.R.' and he had no connection with the crime.

Pressure increased on the police, and the fact that Scotland Yard had seconded two officers may have helped the investigation, but it did not ease the pressure. Who had murdered Mrs Mogano?

A man was seen trying to 'thumb' a lift on the Ryton Road at 6.50 a.m. on 19 January, the day after the murder. When he signalled for a lift he used his left hand and kept his right hand in his pocket. His description did tally in some details with that of a man seen on the afternoon of the murder in a 'phone box near Mrs Mogano's home, and that man's right hand was wrapped in a makeshift bandage. He was seen as far away as the Dunstable (Bedfordshire) area in an orange-coloured lorry, which was loaded with metal girders and thought to be travelling towards London. Police forces throughout the country helped follow up this lead by checking with local transport firms.

Two weeks after the murder, the police were still hoping to find the round-headed hammer believed to have been used to batter Mrs Mogano. Householders were again asked to search their back gardens in the hope it would come to light. Tests had been carried out and it seemed fairly certain they were looking for a two-pound, round-headed hammer.

Police also launched an appeal to anyone who had used the 'phone box where the 'man with the makeshift bandage' had been seen making a call late on the afternoon of the murder. Although the public response had been encouraging, it was still felt that someone was withholding a vital piece of information.

Sixteen days after the murder, the 'man with the makeshift bandage' was traced to London. Police officers from Coventry travelled to London to accompany him back for questioning. Scotland Yard's mobile squad had traced him to a lodging house in Peckham. His home was apparently Coventry though.

After more useful information, detectives were able to create an accurate picture of Mrs Mogano's afternoon routines, which provoked further questions, especially as she would often leave home for a while. She was out for three afternoons in the week before the murder. It was thought that as she was seen with a paper-wrapped parcel that these were dancing shoes and she was receiving some private tuition. Police were following this up closely. Results from lab tests of the 'phone box and directory did not move the investigation forward as the blood found was of the same group as both Mrs Mogano and a police officer who had been attacked in that 'phone box some weeks previously.

The net was widening, with inquiries being followed up all around England, although the thought that the murderer might have been local had not been ruled out. However, the man brought back to Coventry from the Peckham boarding house did not help the inquiry, and it appeared he was not the man seen leaving the 'phone box in Radford on the afternoon of the murder. He was able to make a statement but this mainly centred around the descriptions he could give of other hitchhikers he met travelling from Coventry to London.

Police forces around the country contributed to what was described as a 'mass of statements and reports' and gave some 'promising new leads' but DSupt Edmunds still felt the investigation was hampered by someone withholding that vital piece of information so desperately needed. Five people had come forward to say they had used the 'phone box where the 'man with the makeshift bandage' had been seen, and their fingerprints were taken for elimination purposes; however, the identity of the 'man with the makeshift bandage' was still not clear. But some more details were emerging of Mrs Mogano's activities in the week leading up to the murder. The police said they were not expecting to find anything to Mrs Mogano's discredit but wished to fill in the gaps to see if any new 'lines of inquiry' could be found. DSupt Edmunds said, 'She may not have had a secret at all. Her trips may have been ordinary visits to town but there are still some blank spaces.'

Meanwhile, police had checked up on local men with a history of violence but nothing was uncovered that was linked to the case. Quite a few local folk had found quite a few hammers and general pieces of iron in their gardens and had handed them in. Tests were carried out but to no avail. And the driver of the lorry who gave the 'man with the makeshift bandage' a lift could not be found, nor the man himself.

DSupt Edmunds returned to London for a conference and had prolonged meetings with Coventry City Detectives on his return. A month had passed since the murder and more than 2,000 homes in the Radford district alone had been visited. Each household completed the questionnaire. The possibilities of an arrest were beginning to look remote. The resumed inquest into Mrs Mogano's death was again adjourned in late February.

The 'electricity meter man' – who was reportedly at large in Oxford, Middlesex and Dorset as well as London, Birmingham and Coventry – was not traced, nor was the 'man with the makeshift bandage'. Several men were interviewed under caution but none charged.

Over 10,000 men and women were interviewed in the inquiry. But had he slipped through the net?

A month after the murder, one of the 10,000 became the focus of the inquiry: a bushy eye-browed bath salts salesman who had been questioned earlier in the inquiry. Further information was received by the police, who became anxious to trace him, but he and his girlfriend appeared to have completely vanished from their lodgings in Leicester. They were not traced.

The inquiry stalled. Mrs Mogano was cremated at Canley Crematorium. Mr Mogano died in March 1986.

ELIZABETH THOMAS, LAUGHARNE, 1953

Coronation year, 1953, saw its share of tragedy, and the small community of Laugharne (pronounced 'Larne') in Carmarthen, South Wales, lost their most-celebrated resident, Dylan Thomas, though he actually died in New York. About ten months before this, another Thomas died in Laugharne, and caught the headlines for quite a different reason. On Saturday 10 January, Miss Elizabeth Thomas, a seventy-eight-year-old retired schoolteacher, was murdered in her home in Clifton Street, Laugharne.

The crime was discovered at around 6.15 p.m. by Mr Ronald Jones, who was passing Miss Thomas's cottage and heard a woman screaming. Mr Jones thought that she called the name 'Harry' but was not sure; he also heard two or three thuds as if somebody was impacting on a solid surface. But he only recognised a woman's voice, and thought that by the way she was screaming she was trying to ward off an attack.

Mr Jones ran to the adjacent Belle View Garage for assistance and the proprietor, Jacques de Schoolmeester, with Police Sergeant Thomas Morgans, who happened to be there at the time, quickly went to Miss Thomas's house. They gained entry through a ground-floor window and found Miss Thomas lying on the floor injured. A doctor was summoned and an ambulance called; the police became more formally involved the following morning when Miss Thomas died.

The Chief Constable, Mr T. Hubert Lewis, asked for the 'Yard'. DSupt Reginald Spooner and DS Ernest Millen arrived in Carmarthen shortly before midnight on 11 January. They met with Mr Lewis and Superintendent David Jones early the following morning.

On 16 January 1953, George Roberts, a forty-six-year-old odd-job man of Ferry House, Laugharne, was charged with murder and appeared before St Clears Magistrates' Court on 19 January 1953. He was remanded in custody until 27 January, and the only evidence given was by Superintendent Jones regarding his arrest and charging.

The charge was said to be based on a confession with some supporting evidence. George had been deaf and mute since birth. In those days this could and did leave folk illiterate and as this was a largely rural community George's development had been left wanting. However, by all accounts he appeared to be of normal intelligence and reasoning.

Miss Thomas's house was in the centre of a block of five cottages towards the end of Clifton Street, a continuation of King Street, which was the main street of the town. There were gardens to the rear of the cottages, which was the route the murderer took to escape.

When PS Morgans and the two men arrived at the cottage, faint moans were heard and they tried to attract Miss Thomas's attention by shouting and rattling the front door. They tried this for several minutes and then the light in the front room appeared to go out.

PS Morgans looked through the keyhole and saw the top of a cap on the head of somebody in a bent position in the hall, though he could not say whether this was a man, woman or child. He heard the sound of what he thought was a metallic bucket falling inside the passage, suggesting the assailant was still on the premises. He later learnt the cap would have been near to where Miss Thomas's head was. PS Morgans pulled down a window and climbed in. He then let the other two men in through the front door.

The three men found Miss Thomas in the hallway, lying on her back on the floor. Her legs were slightly bent and she was moving her arms about and moaning. She lay towards the centre of the hall and there was no apparent interference to her clothing.

PS Morgans remained at the scene of the crime. The lamp was relit by Mr Jones; the glass of the lamp was still warm so the lamp had been put out by the intruder. Pieces of comb, a hair slide, another comb, a lower denture, and pieces of wall plaster were found near the body. A bucket containing newspapers stood on the mat outside the door of the living room and just beyond this was a bucket of water, some of which had been spilled, partly moistening Miss Thomas's clothing. There was a third bucket containing coal and ashes which had been knocked over. There was also a piece of wood, with strands of what seemed to be human hair attached, propped up against the wall.

PS Morgans found the door of the living room wide open, and the back door of the house was also open, resting on its top hinge. Mr de Schoolmeester went to telephone for assistance. Doctor David Hughes attended the house at 6.35 p.m., saw Miss Thomas's injuries and ordered her removal to hospital. Miss Thomas was unable to answer any questions about her attacker.

Dr Hughes was specific about his time of arrival being 6.35 p.m. and he had received the call at 6.21 p.m. He was sure of the time because he made a note – he had arranged an operation for 6.30 p.m. and was concerned about the time.

The Ambulance Control Centre in Carmarthen received a summons at 6.40 p.m. and directed attendance. Miss Thomas arrived at West Wales Hospital in Carmarthen at 7.05 p.m. On arrival, Miss Thomas was seen by Dr John Evans, who found her suffering from a number of injuries. She was given a blood transfusion but she died at 9.10 a.m. the next morning (11 January). Dr Evans confirmed death.

The post-mortem examination was carried out on 12 January 1953, by Dr Charles Freezer, Home Office Pathologist. Identification of the body was by Mr Gomer Perkins (her nephew), PS Morgans, and Dr Evans.

The injuries were:

Fracture of the right forearm.

Fracture of the skull.

Deep bruising in the abdomen.

Three punctured wounds, two over the breast bone and one in the abdominal wall.

Four puncture wounds in the back, in the left flank, deeper than those in the chest and having sharp edges and tapering extremities.

A superficial bruise in front of the left knee.

A tear inside of the scalp.

His conclusions were that she had been a healthy – although aged – woman who died of shock, which was the cumulative result of the multiple injuries she received, the most serious of which was the fracture of the skull. The amount of blood loss had not been of a dangerous degree.

The puncture wounds were all superficial bar one in her back, which had pricked the lung. There was no sexual agenda apparent. Although not in his report, Dr Freezer said his opinion was that the stab wounds had been caused by a sharp pointed instrument, such as a knife.

Miss Thomas's next of kin were three nephews – Gomer, Gordon and John Perkins – who also lived in Laugharne. She lived alone, and since the death of her sister (the Perkins's mother) in October 1932, went to their house from Monday to Friday to prepare their evening meals. She would arrive at around 4.00 p.m. and go home at around 8.30 p.m. On Saturdays, she would not call until 7.00 p.m. and would stay until 8.30 p.m. On Sundays, she would call at their house at 4.00 p.m. and stay for a couple of hours.

The nephew closest to her was Gomer Perkins, who had actually been looking after her since she suffered an illness about a year before. Since then she had lived in one room. He said she would usually light the oil lamp and draw the curtains as evening came on. He added that whenever he called, the front door was on the latch and he would walk straight in. Mr Perkins said that the only time that he knew it was locked was early in the morning or in the evenings when she would visit him and his brothers. Miss Thomas had last visited her three nephews on the evening of 9 January, the day before the crime, when she seemed to be in good health and spoke of seeing them again the following evening.

She told Gomer Perkins about a month before her death that she had some money in the house; he had kept this to himself, but when he was called to her house later, he told PS Morgans. This money amounted to £271.

1953 Mr and Mrs Phillips' shop just by the car: Miss Thomas's house opposite. (ASSI 84/157 Courtesy The National Archives)

2011 Miss Thomas's house is visible, just level with the further telegraph pole on the right side.

1953 Miss Thomas's house in the terrace on the right. (ASSI 84/157 Courtesy The National Archives)

2011 Little change; just modern roads and more motor cars.

The two persons – other than her nephews – who appeared to have been friendly with Miss Thomas were John Phillips and his wife, Elisabeth, who kept a small general store across the road. They said that she had called into the shop at 5.00 p.m. on the evening of the attack, and she had stayed for about fifteen minutes. Mrs Phillips was more specific about this and may have been the last person to see Miss Thomas alive.

Miss Thomas's immediate neighbours were Mr Theophilus Howell and Miss Elizabeth Davies. Like Miss Thomas, they live alone and had known her for many years. They both said they saw her on 10 January. Miss Davies said that Miss Thomas would always lock her front door when she left the house and would carry the key with her.

Miss Thomas's other neighbours at Nos 1 and 5 Clifton Street were Mr Harry Wellstead and his family, and Mr Edward Williams and his family. Apart from Mr Williams, who saw her during the afternoon of 10 January, neither could tell the police much about her. She did tend to live as a semi-recluse, and occupied just the one room of her cottage. The other downstairs room on the opposite side of the hall was closed and secured. The stairway leading from the living room to the first floor of the house was covered with cobwebs and clearly no one had been any further than the living room and hall for a good while. The house was described as filthy, with fleas and rats in residence; upstairs a bed was found full of maggots. The sanitary arrangements were primitive and situated in the back garden, water was drawn from a communal pump and the only lighting was by one oil lamp.

When the house was searched, small sums of money were found in various places in the living room. This was apart from the £271 Mr Perkins had discussed, which had been taken for safekeeping by Superintendent Jones.

Superintendent Jones had instigated preliminary inquiries following the discovery of the crime, and it soon came to light that George was seen in the area at the time of the crime. With DS Frederick Jones, he went to George's address at 1.00 a.m. (11 January) and questioned him through his uncle, Lewis Roberts. His account of his movements was not satisfactory and because of the difficulty of questioning him, he was taken to Carmarthen Police Station.

He was asked to dress in the clothing that he had worn the previous day, which was later taken for examination together with other items of his clothing.

George lived with three uncles – Lewis, David and John Roberts – in a cottage known as Ferry House, Laugharne. None were married. This is half a mile away from Miss Thomas's cottage at the foot of the cliffs by the sea. George was the son of his uncles' sister, Mary Ann Roberts, who had died in 1945.

George Roberts was born on 2 January 1902 at Laugharne, so was fifty-one years of age and not forty-six as recorded elsewhere in his records. He had been deaf since birth and since leaving school at thirteen years had been employed as a handyman by various inhabitants of Laugharne. He was known to almost all of the residents of Laugharne (about 960) and referred to as 'Budda' – there did not seem a consensus as to how this should be spelt.

He had not been in trouble with the police before and was described as being a 'perfectly good character'. However, there was some suggestion of an indecent assault on a young married lady at the time, which I will discuss later.

Witness statements were collected that described his movements and activities on 10 January. Mrs Constance David had employed George for nearly thirty years and each day he would do odd jobs for her. She was quite confident of her safety and would even leave the door open for him. On 10 January, he arrived at her house, 'The Cross' (or The Cors), at around 8.00 a.m. and left at 11.00 a.m. He then went to the house of Miss Elizabeth Vaughan, Cliff Cottage, Laugharne – for whom he had also done casual work for the last thirty years. Here, he had a midday meal and left at around 2.30 p.m. After this, he went home where he was seen by all three of his uncles. John Roberts said he got there at around 3.00 p.m. and left again at around 4.30 p.m.

Shortly after leaving home, he met Mr Thomas Langdon and intimated that he wished to get some batteries for his torch. He guided him to 'Ebsworth's Garage' and then to 'Belle View Garage'; Mr Randall Lloyd corroborated this. Both men then left and were seen by Mr Aguila Evans going towards the church. This route would have taken them past the front of the Miss Thomas's house. Mr Langdon said George had accompanied him to the church where he (Mr Langdon) had work to do, so George walked back alone toward the centre of the town.

But Mr Langdon's job did not take long and he caught up with him walking by Ebsworth's Garage at around 4.25 p.m., but George waved his hand and walked into Miss Elisabeth Lewis' house: her door was open. Miss Lewis speaks of him calling on her at around 4.30 p.m. and of showing her a new pair of woollen gloves he had been given as a present. He left soon after and went along Clifton Street. The significance of this is that he turned back the way he had come from the church, and in the direction of Miss Thomas's house, and without Mr Langdon. He was seen here by two witnesses, but one of the witness's evidence has vanished. DSupt Spooner gives an account of the evidence offered by Mr Gwilym Hughes but his deposition and presence at Glamorgan Assizes is not recorded. Mr Cyrus Morgans could relate that he saw George at 4.50 p.m., but back at the garage where he had bought the batteries.

George appears to have gone along Clifton Street towards Miss Thomas's house. Mrs Phillips said Miss Thomas left her shop (opposite) at around 5.15 p.m. and she saw her cross the road to her own home. At about this time, she saw George standing outside her shop. Between then and around 5.55 p.m., he was seen standing outside the house next door to the Phillips' shop by seven different witnesses. Timings ranged from 5.00 p.m. to 5.50 p.m. All the witnesses who saw him outside the Phillips' shop describe him as standing on the edge of the pavement.

According to DSupt Spooner's report, George was not seen again until 6.15 p.m. – but was anyone passing or in view of the pavement outside of Mr Phillips' shop from 6.00 to 6.15 p.m.? Could anyone say they passed the spot but did not see him? DSupt

Spooner actually recorded that 'Roberts was not seen again until 6.15 p.m. when he passed by the house of Mr Walter Edmunds next door to Phillips' and directly opposite the deceased's'.

It does seem as though there was an extraordinary amount of witnesses – seven in all. But between 6.00 p.m. and 6.15 p.m. he is seen by no one. But this does not prove he was in the house of Miss Thomas.

A Mr Arthur Jenkins made a statement to say that he saw a man answering George's description at 6.15 p.m., but he said it was dark. And although he knew George well, he did not recognise the man he saw as he could not see the man's face. And this showed that whilst passing the scene of crime, he did so on the opposite side of the road to Miss Thomas's where the other witnesses report seeing George. So, with no witnesses to record the contrary, George may have remained in the same spot where he was seen by the seven witnesses up to 5.50 p.m. and then throughout the crucial period from 6.00 to 6.15 p.m. He would not have heard the commotion in Miss Thomas's house, but it is possible he saw someone enter. In fact, as he was possibly at this spot for the prolonged period from 5.00 p.m. until he was seen to walk away from the spot at 6.15 p.m., it would have been highly likely he saw someone enter Miss Thomas's property. But communications were so basic in sign language that extracting any information from him would have been impossible. He was unable to read so could not follow the most elementary instructions. Therefore, as a witness he could not have been examined or cross-examined in court. Of course, sign language existed in those days, but he had not received training in its use; most of the villagers who communicated with him did so in a most rudimentary way.

According to Mr Jenkins, he spoke to the man he saw, saying 'goodnight'. The man did not reply but turned up his coat collar with both hands as he passed by. Mr Jenkins puts the time of this as just after 6.15 p.m. This is unlikely to be George because most of the witnesses (himself and his uncles included) say he wore a light-coloured cap, yet Mr Jenkins said the man he saw did not wear anything on his head.

George was next seen further down the street towards the centre of the town by Mrs Gweneth Lewis between 6.25 p.m. and 6.30 p.m. At 6.40 p.m., he was seen in Victoria Street by Thomas Rowles. DSupt Spooner reports that 'the witnesses to Roberts' movements between 6.15 p.m. and 6.40 p.m. show that he was on his way home, from opposite the scene of the crime where he had been seen loitering.'

Was he loitering? It is impossible to say because of the communication difficulties between him and the other witnesses, police *et al*. Later, I can discuss how the police attempted to overcome this.

George's uncles, David and John, said he got home at around 6.30 p.m. and the other uncle, Lewis, said that when he arrived home at around 6.45 p.m., his nephew was there. They retired between 9.30 and 9.45 p.m.

When George was seen 'loitering' opposite Miss Thomas's house, it was dark and the street lighting poor. But one would be naturally cautious about saying any one of the witnesses made a mistake about the identity or the time or date.

The word 'loitering' seems to take its exit as DSupt Spooner reports on the preceding few weeks of life in Laugharne. However, he produces a catalogue of people who say they saw George 'hanging around'. And these sightings were not concentrated on only one part of the town. It is possible that he had intentions that were not wholly innocent, but this is at the negative end of supposition. And without any 'facts', one should be swayed by what the residents of Laugharne said about him; or more to the point, what they did not say about him – a bad word. No one in any of the statements says anything negative about him. He had never been known to be violent or show a loss of temper; he was trustworthy and did not take any liberties with what he was entrusted with.

One report was of some form of sexual assault or harassment, which I will return to presently, but there is plenty of suggestion in the way the police conducted the inquiry that they were suspicious of George so they would go out and find 'something on him'. So much was this the case that after a long list of his 'suspicious' behaviour, in which only one person mentioned his light-coloured cap, PS Morgans is highlighted by DSupt Spooner as saying the assailant wore a light-coloured cap. No doubt DSupt Spooner was disappointed when PS Morgans said he was unsure as to whether he saw a man, woman or child. The lamp had been extinguished, and, of course, George could not have heard the commotion occurring outside of Miss Thomas's cottage as PS Morgans *et al.* rattled the door and shouted.

'The time factor is of importance, but inevitably witnesses are in most cases approximate and vary a little one with the other, although not by much ...' reported DSupt Spooner. So is it possible that when it is reported that no witnesses saw George between 6.00 and 6.15 p.m. that this could be 5.55 and 6.10 p.m. or some other permutation of the time? Could the police prove his whereabouts was unaccounted for between the 6.00 and 6.15 p.m. when he reappeared, but by then Miss Thomas, according to Mr Jones, Mr de Schoolmeester and PS Morgans, had already been attacked?

Both Mr Walter Edmunds and his brother Benjamin said that they were milking in the cowshed at 6.00 p.m. (which would be before Miss Thomas was attacked), when they heard a crying noise coming from the direction of Clifton Street but paid no attention to it. PS Morgans also put the time at around 6.15 p.m. when he was at the house, but Mr de Schoolmeester and Mr Jones could only say that it was just after 6.00 p.m. Dr Hughes said he received a relayed telephone call at 6.21 p.m., which suggests that PS Morgans *et al.* arrived at the house just before 6.15 p.m. But there are many factors to be taken into account: Mr Jones hearing the screams, running to the garage, explaining the situation, approaching the house, calling her name, seeing someone in the house with a cap on, rattling the door, climbing in through the window and so on. Meanwhile, George has been seen at 6.15 p.m. only about a minute's walk away.

Portrait of George Roberts.

Statements were taken from two thirteen-year-old schoolgirls, Mary Edwards and Dilys Williams, who had visited Mary's aunt, Mrs Gweneth Lewis, at her house in Clifton Street. They left together and, according to Mary, the clock showed 6.10 p.m. Both appeared to have arrived at Miss Thomas's house at about the same time as PS Morgans and the other two men. After seeing the sergeant get through the window and open the door, they became frightened and returned to her aunt. According to Miss Williams, it was between 6.10 and 6.15 p.m. when they got back. She estimates this time by the 6.15 p.m. Pendine bus.

Mrs Lewis confirmed the two girls left her house at 6.10 p.m. and returned about ten minutes later. It was after this, between 6.25 p.m. and 6.30 p.m. that she saw George. Mrs Lewis's husband, Thomas, confirms all of the times given by his wife about her niece and her friend, stating that he knows the girls left his house at around 6.10 p.m. because he looked at the clock and remarked that he had missed the news – but if he had missed the news does that prove necessarily that it was 6.10 p.m.?

Mr Theophilus Howell, who lived next door to Miss Thomas, said that he was listening to the wireless until the sports news came on at 6.15 p.m. He then went to his bedroom to change his clothing, and heard voices in front of his house. He saw the witnesses, Benjamin Edmunds and Noel Lewis, come out of Miss Thomas's house.

This asks more questions than it answers. If PS Morgans *et al.* got to the house at 6.15 p.m., gained entry and called help – this all taking, perhaps, two or three minutes – then when did the witnesses seen by Mr Howell actually *arrive* at the cottage?

So, considering all of these times and the sequence of incidents, the question emerges of whether it was possible for George to have escaped from Miss Thomas's house in time for Mr Edmunds to have seen him when and where he said he did. It also assumes that each and every one of the witnesses had perfectly synchronised watches, clocks, etc.

Miss Thomas's cottage was in the middle of a terrace of five. Each of their back gardens were divided by hedges. At one end of the terrace there was a side entrance with a path leading out onto Clifton Street. The hedges were generally partly broken down and there was a path from the bottom of Miss Thomas's garden, through the gaps in the hedges that joined a path which led to the side of No. 5 and out onto Clifton Street. So it was possible, indeed probable, that whoever attacked Miss Thomas escaped this way.

The police made some timings of whether the attacker could have reached the point where Mr Walter Edmunds said he saw George, on the opposite side of the road to Miss Thomas's cottage. From the back of Miss Thomas's cottage over the back gardens, through the side entrance and out onto Clifton Street took a minute. To cover the full 120 yards from the back of the cottage, over the gardens and out onto Clifton Street – then across the road –would take a minute and a quarter. According to the police, George would have had ample time to have done this. But why cross the road and take time moving on?

There would, of course, at just after 6.00 p.m. on a January evening, be almost complete darkness in the back garden and anyone unfamiliar with the layout may have had some difficulty. In one's own house when the 'trip-switch' goes and the place is in darkness, then there is usually some difficulty navigating until the lights go on again – and that is in one's own house. However, as the police pointed out, not only was George familiar with the layout, he also had a torch, complete with fresh batteries. According to Mr de Schoolmeester, Miss Thomas had recently bought a new torch, but who else did he sell a new torch to?

On 12 January 1953, DS Glynne Jones went to George's home and took possession of two torches, one green and the other brown and chromium plated. Both contained two Vidor batteries, but those in the green torch were newer. According to Lewis Roberts, the green torch belonged to his nephew.

The police wondered if George had reasons, other than the batteries being flat, for buying new batteries for his torch. If he had an ulterior motive and use for his torch then he made no attempt to hide it. Nevertheless, 'there can be no doubt from the evidence that he had it (the torch) in his possession when Miss Thomas was attacked, and he could have used it in his escape through the back gardens in the darkness.'

In none of the other statements or depositions is there any record of any other witness being asked if they possessed a torch, or had taken it out with them that evening.

The police were keen to trace any weapons they thought had been used and the knife was their priority. The house George lived in was searched, but apart from a rusty old jack-knife, no weapon was found. Dr Freezer needed to remind the police that the wounds were caused by a sharp, pointed knife. It is unclear if they had lost sight of this or simply bombarded him with everything found answering to the description of 'knife' no matter how unlikely the possibility; for instance, a pair of tweezers found in the bathroom. Some inquiries were to see if George had ever been seen with a knife during the course of his various employments, but no one said he had been.

On 16 January 1953, the police took statements from four young people: Trevor Brown, David Davies, Pamela Rees and Sheila Adams. They were all between thirteen and nineteen years of age and spent time together walking along the cliffs near where George lived. According to the two boys, they were together on the cliffs and they saw him. They made signs that he, Mr Brown, wanted to sharpen his pencil. George put his hand inside his inner jacket pocket and pulled out a knife which he gave to him. He sharpened his pencil and gave the knife back. The knife was described as being as 'sharp as a razor' on the side used, but less sharp on the other edge; it had a sharp point. The blade was 7–8 inches long with a handle of 3–4 inches long. It was about an inch wide at the bottom of the blade and tapered to a point. It was not of the loosely described 'pen knife' or folding type.

Trevor Brown added that this was the first time had seen George with a knife. Since then he had seen him with the same knife three or four times, each time sharpening it on a stone on the cliff walk.

David Davies confirmed borrowing the knife, and his description of the knife was similar to Trevor Brown's.

Pamela Rees and Sheila Adams, although in the company of the two boys, did not see the knife, though Pamela said she had seen George sharpening sticks with a knife. Sheila Adams did not see the knife, but said that the boys described it to her.

So witness evidence could not really help, but forensic evidence was gathered. A thorough search was made for any fingerprints but only one possibly unexplainable impression was found, and closer examination showed it belonged to Mr Jones. It was found on the oil lamp that he had relit when he gained access with PS Morgans. A footprint was discovered on the stone floor in the hall, so the entire section was lifted and sent to Scotland Yard for analysis. It was compared with the wellingtons George wore on the evening of the crime, but it did not match. So the footwear of the other twenty-four people who had been in Miss Thomas's house after the attack were checked. Only two people's footwear showed any resemblance to the pattern found: the police photographer DS Frederick Jones and Dr Hughes.

On George's clothing was found some fragments of what was thought to be distemper from Miss Thomas house. However, the white fragments were not consistent with anything found in the cottage, whereas the green residue was. But this was in the days before the mass culture of Do-It-Yourself and, in the case of a seventy-eight-year-old lady, it is more likely to belong to a batch used by the local painter and decorator, and there is no sign this line of inquiry was pursued. So the forensic evidence did not support the idea that George had even been at the cottage. Some blood was found in the pocket of his mackintosh, but he had cut a finger some days previous.

All the police had was a sighting of George opposite Miss Thomas's house before what was thought to be the time of the attack, and sightings of him walking away from the area after the attack. And even then the timings were vague. There was no proof he had been in Miss Thomas's cottage – the 'light cap' seen by PS Morgans was far too indistinct and seen momentarily in poor or little light and, by PS Morgans' own deposition, it was not possible to say if the wearer was a man, woman or child.

So it would be of use to consider what George actually said to the police in questioning. But first it might be of help to consider what he said in comparison to what another witness said – the pathologist.

The attack on Miss Thomas took place late afternoon or early evening on Saturday 10 January, which was the date she was taken to hospital. She died in the morning of Sunday 11th and a post-mortem examination was carried out the following day. The post-mortem suggests two phases of attack: the first as blows to the head with a heavy blunt instrument, and the second punctures/stabbings to the trunk with a sharp knife. Both of these phases were, albeit scantily, described in George's deposition. However, there could be described as being a further or preliminary phase of the attack, probably made with the same heavy blunt instrument as the blows on her head. Miss Thomas had tried to defend herself by holding her right arm up – the result of which was heavy bruising on her wrist and in fact her forearm was broken (both radius and ulna) in this phase of the attack.

What this means is that two distinct 'weapons' were used – a heavy blunt instrument and a knife. The heavy blunt instrument could well have been a piece of wood Miss Thomas put at the bottom of the back door to stop drafts – it was found adjacent to her, propped up against the wall. It had what appeared to be human blood on it and some hair adhering to this. This means the question of disposal of the weapons presents itself: no attempt was made to conceal the blunt instrument used, but the knife was never formally identified nor found.

Dealing with so-called 'confession evidence' had always been a problem for the criminal law. Although it could sway a jury, it did not really satisfy the demands of the law, and even though the standard caution could be given to a suspect about anything they say, there were instances where police officers would swear under oath a prisoner made a confession, say, in the back of a car on the way to a police station. The practice was said to be rife until the Police and Criminal Evidence Act (PACE) of the 1980s, and so widespread was this that it even attracted a name: 'Verballing'. This could be considered under what was referred to as 'noble cause' corruption but was still not lawful. Under PACE, any such evidence was inadmissible.

But this was years before PACE, so what did George 'confess' to?

A Mrs Ceridwen Beddoe-Davies, Court Interpreter and Interpreter for the Llanelly and West Wales Mission for the Deaf and Dumb, was asked to help. At 11.15 a.m. on 11 January, George was interviewed by DS Jones with the help of Mrs Davies. George did say he saw the deceased on her doorstep at around 4.00 p.m. on the day and acknowledged her. He arrived home at 5.00 p.m. and did not go out again. When told that he was seen near Miss Thomas's house between 5.30 and 5.45 p.m., he said that he was not there but at home.

On 12 January, George was examined by Dr Evans for signs of injury, and DS Millen was present for this examination. He found on his right leg below the knee three small abrasions close together, and a small abrasion on the upper right arm. Dr Evans said he thought the injuries were recent. George's explanation was that the mark on his arm was caused by his clothing rubbing and that on the leg by hitting it with an axe. At the same time, Dr Evans took blood samples but they did not prove of any use. Police Constable Gordon Bennett, who had knowledge of the sign alphabet and sign language generally, was also present for the doctor's examination.

DSupt Spooner and Superintendent Jones, together with Mrs Davies, interviewed George on 13 January. Also present was Mrs Davies' husband, William. He was deaf, but was fully conversant with the sign language and manual alphabet, especially in dealing with deaf people.

George had the added difficulty of being illiterate and understood more by signs than anything else. So the seriousness of the crime, and the necessity for no misunderstanding by George as to the questions put to him, prompted the decision to use the services of both Mr and Mrs Davies. The interview took the form of question and answer. The questions were framed by DSupt Spooner, recorded by Superintendent Jones and then put to George by Mrs Davies, observed by her husband. He denied any association with the crime, but his answers were contradictory and his explanations unsatisfactory. But this conceals a possible, even probable, lack of understanding by the investigator, interpreter or subject.

As to the injury on his leg, he said he did this by hitting it with a scythe, but he told DS Millen he did it with an axe. The police attitude towards this was suspicion. However, he denied ever having been in Miss Thomas's house or garden or those next door. It was known through what other witnesses said that he had been in the gardens. The comment by DSupt Spooner was 'this was untrue'. Who is to say he fully understood the question or that the reply he gave was not misunderstood? George spoke of Mr Langdon on the afternoon of 10 January, and of going to buy a battery for his torch. George says that he and this man were in each other's company all the time until they eventually parted in the centre of the town, when he went home and the other man went to a pub. The interrogators drew attention to the fact that he varied his times 'considerably'. He did rely on the town hall clock but other witnesses did not, but there is no recorded check that the town hall clock kept time accurately.

George said he saw Mrs Thomas on her doorstep at 6.20 p.m., but he changed this time to 5.50 p.m. Again one has to question the accuracy of what he perceived was asked of him and what was perceived of his reply.

It could not be proved that George had kicked over the bucket PS Morgans heard fall over. In fact, George said the injury to his leg had been sustained as he was chopping wood, and the police made an issue of the fact that he did not mention this to whoever he was working for, yet when he cut his finger he complained of this fact to Mrs David. At no time had he complained to her that he had cut his leg whilst chopping firewood, but it is an assumption that this is relevant. However, what is relevant was that the measurement from the bottom to the top of the bucket did not correspond with the measurement from the sole of George's foot to where the injury was on his leg.

But there was more 'evidence' which was considered 'inconsistent' regarding the injury to his leg. Miss Ethel Watkins said that on 15 January George called to see her. He told her of his visit to the police station and then showed her some small cuts in his calf, which he said he had received by cutting a hedge. But Miss Elizabeth Vaughan said George never complained of having cut his leg, and his uncle David Roberts states that neither he nor his brothers had been told by George that he had hurt himself recently. Perhaps Miss Watkins would give him tea and sympathy and the others did not!

The interview ended and he was not detained, but on Sunday 18 January, he called at the police station and at 12.45 p.m., he was seen there by DSupt Spooner and DS Millen. His demeanour had changed and he looked worried. He seems to have indicated that he wanted to say something. DSupt Spooner produced some photographs of the locale. He pointed at a house and DS Millen gave George a pencil and paper: he drew a sketch of a row of houses, and drew a figure of himself outside the house next door to the shop opposite.

He pointed to the centre house and made several of what DSupt Spooner understood to be thrusting movements. 'Mr Roberts was shown a knife and he nodded his head affirmatively', though it is not clear what he was affirming. George pointed to the centre house again and moved his finger over the houses until he pointed to himself. Then he indicated walking away.

DSupt Spooner sent for PC Bennett who arrived at 1.40 p.m. He was told by DSupt Spooner that he 'believed Roberts wanted to say something and that it might be an admission.' He asked PC Bennett to repeat a series of questions to George and relate his answers back. The proceedings were recorded, DSupt Spooner said:

> When it became evident to me that Roberts was truthfully admitting the murder of Elizabeth Thomas, I caused him to be formally cautioned, but first took the precaution, in view of his disabilities, of giving him to fully understand the seriousness of what he was saying ...

The interview lasted about forty minutes and Mr and Mrs Davies were then sent for to 'put beyond all doubt the accuracy of my interview with Roberts and to ensure that he fully understood everything'.

What followed was, as DSupt Spooner recorded:

> Mrs. Davies alone to repeat, bit by bit, the questions and answers in Sergeant Millen's notebook to Roberts, to see if he understood them and whether they were accurately recorded. Mrs. Davies did so and George was said to have agreed that everything was correct.

At the conclusion of the 'interview' Mr and Mrs Davies read DS Millen's notebook and confirmed that the questions, answers and caution were repeated to George. He was then taken into custody by Superintendent Jones and formally charged with Miss Thomas's murder. He was cautioned and in reply said, 'I understand. That is all I have to say.' Mrs Davies acted as interpreter at this stage also. Mrs Davies said (and her husband agreed) that George was an intelligent man and that there was 'never any doubt that he fully understood everything that she and her husband asked him and was quick with his answers'.

So, no clear eyewitness or forensic evidence, but the police had a confession. Or did they?

Apparently the knife was thrown out to sea, but a big piece of wood found in Miss Thomas's house, which was almost certainly the 'blunt instrument', was left just where it was placed after the attack.

At low tide, a search was made with the aid of mine detectors, but the knife was not found. The cliff face was also searched. The police even used 'drag magnets' under the water of the incoming tide but all to no avail. The currents were said to be strong so it was suggested that the knife could have been absorbed into deep water.

George's confession stated that he stabbed Miss Thomas in both the back and front of the body with a knife; this was consistent with the pathologist's report, as was also his 'admission' of hitting Miss Thomas on the head, and further admissions were that he went into the living room and turned out the lamp. Here, again, this is in keeping with the evidence of PS Morgans, Mr Jones and Mr de Schoolmeester.

DSupt Spooner also said:

> It was thought significant that despite some minutes of violently rattling the front door and shouting by PS Morgans when Miss Thomas was heard to scream, her assailant remained on the premises even seen stooping over her body and turning out the light.

PS Morgans did not describe 'some minutes of violently rattling the front door', he said he tried to open it, but it was locked. He shouted, it is true, and it was clear there was someone outside of the house. But as George was deaf he would not know of this and therefore what DSupt Spooner says is put in doubt by the mere fact that the assailant put out the light – how would George know he needed to do this at this point? If he thought there was money in the house, and hence the attack, then why did he not simply search for the money as he did not know the police (with assistance) were upon him?

Although not a useful factor in determining the guilt for this crime, no motive was identified. 'Mr Roberts himself, in his confession, says he does not know why he killed Miss Thomas.'

Motive is not always altogether clear but it was thought robbery may have been a factor. However, no one, so far as could be discovered, knew Miss Thomas had money in her home. George's needs were not great – he enjoyed 'comic' newspapers and his cigarettes; he had at his home a few pounds which were cared for by his uncle, David. There was also found at his home some £500 in bank notes and silver, but this probably belonged to his uncles. It was discovered that the three uncles and George had a joint bank account, and of some years standing.

So DSupt Spooner recorded that there did not appear to be any reason on George's part to steal. Moreover, there was no history either of conviction or accusation, nor was there any suggestion that he knew of the monies in Miss Thomas's house.

There was some suggestion that George had behaved inappropriately to a female acquaintance. A young married woman with three children, whose husband was away with the Army in Korea, made a statement. However, it does not seem as though the line of inquiry followed by police had resulted in any firm evidence.

The young lady was employed at Brown's Hotel, Laugharne, as a general assistant, and had been there for thirteen years. She was mainly employed to serve in the bar. According to her, George was at one time a frequent visitor, though for about four weeks he had not been in the bar.

On 27 December 1952, he was seen in the 'smoke room' at around 8.30 p.m. He was said to 'nudge the young lady to draw attention to his making indecent gestures to another girl behind her back'. Later, when the bar closed at 10.00 p.m., all the customers left except George and he then bought her 'several sherries and then made similar indecent gestures to her. She says that he then held her breasts, put his hand over her private parts and also 'endeavoured to put it (his hand) under her skirt'.

The lady said she quickly withdrew from George's proximity and went into the hotel kitchen away from the public area. She added that George remained in the bar area, but eventually she made her way home. There does not seem to be any record of how this incident was resolved – perhaps a male colleague finished clearing the bar and locked up etc. – nor is there any mention of police follow up. It is also recorded that this had not been an isolated incident, but the history did not come from the lady, so one is left wondering.

DSupt Spooner did interview the lady's sister and her mother, although not the lady in question. The term 'on many occasions' is related by DSupt Spooner, as well as the phrase 'exposed his person to her.' One cannot help wondering though, that if the incident of 27 December was the latest in a series of incidents, why was she, after the other customers in the bar had left, indulging in 'several sherries' with him. This lady also said that George had a bad temper. Both the lady's sister and mother did not seem to be perturbed about the stories, but, in the 1950s, women had to tolerate far worse behaviour from men than they do today.

Another report of another lady threatened with a knife was recorded by the police, but on interview this proved not to be true, though she did say he had a violent temper and was violently inclined. This again revolves around the Carmarthen pub visits and it may have been the case that he did not tolerate alcohol too well. But little of this was pursued by the police, save to say that inquiries were made about George's drinking sessions, but most people said he had not been seen drinking for about a month before Miss Thomas's attack.

The police, then, were attaching some importance to George's apparent change of behaviour in the month previous to Miss Thomas's attack. He did say he had stopped drinking, or rather that he did not drink. The fact that several (and more than I have recorded) witnesses saw him opposite Miss Thomas's house, outside the house next to Mr and Mrs Phillips' shop between 5.30 and 6.00 p.m. does seem strange. But did anyone see him between 6.00 and 6.15 p.m. or was he no longer there? As DSupt Spooner said in his report that 'all sorts of things might be inferred from this but it does not amount to proof.' But he does make a curious observation:

Whatever may have made Mr Roberts attack Miss Thomas, then the attack was not completed. Her resistance and screams [the police's comment] were probably responsible for this. The injuries to her head were undoubtedly caused by the piece of wood, in an attempt either to subdue her or quieten her before he made his escape.

This seems to have been inferred from his 'confession' but is speculative to say the least. George was deaf and if in the course of attacking Miss Thomas he tried to 'quieten' her then it is difficult to understand how he knew of the screaming or of his need for imminent departure – he would not have heard the commotion outside the front door. And even if he could sense 'the vibes' of Miss Thomas screaming then he would have been in a highly excitable state and it is unclear whether this would have impeded this sense of the vibration of sound waves deaf people are said to experience.

When four people – George and his three uncles – share a house, there may be more than one coat hanging up in the hall. As it was January, the police found quite a few, but two were selected for further examination. This is because there was some disagreement among witnesses as to what type of mackintosh George was wearing that night. His uncles say he left the house in a blue mackintosh, but some of the witnesses who saw him say he was wearing a light-ish mackintosh. The police found the two that loosely fitted both descriptions and they were of a similar size. However, in one of the coats was a pair of gloves which matched the description given by Miss Lewis and also there was a Christmas card addressed to 'George', which suggested that this mackintosh was the one usually worn by George.

And it was the light rather than the blue garment that seemed to fit most criteria so was sent for laboratory analysis. The result of the analysis was that the mackintosh (and the jacket he wore under it) bore a material similar to that found in the hall of Miss Thomas's house. But the report said just that: 'similar'.

Blood samples found on George's clothing were too small for grouping, but he did give a blood specimen when asked. This did not take the investigation forward. All of Miss Thomas's clothing were stained with her own blood.

DSupt Spooner felt that this evidence supported the argument that George was wearing this mackintosh at the time of the crime, and that the gloves were his – neither of which he denied. And he added that a spot of blood found in the pocket could suggest this is where he put the knife after the attack, though with the size of the blood specimen found in the pocket, this does stretch credibility.

So the Director of Public Prosecution became involved and George appeared before St Clears Magistrates' Court on 19 January 1953. He was remanded until 27 January, and further remanded until 4 February, before another remand until 12 February.

The case came before St Clear Magistrates on Tuesday 24 February. Several attempts were made through the court deaf and dumb interpreter, by means of mime and sign language, to make George understand the charge, but these were ineffective. George was defended by Mr Myer Cohen, solicitor, Cardiff; Mr E. C. Jones was the Director of Public Prosecutions.

The main issues in court were as described, but I can reiterate from time to time; the first point of the prosecution was the large piece of wood found next to Miss Thomas's body: 'it was found to have hair adhering to it, similar to the hair of the old lady. There is no doubt ... that was the weapon which was used in the attack.'

And regarding George's raincoat:

On a raincoat worn by the accused that evening was a patch of green plaster and distemper which a forensic witness will say was similar to the distemper on the lower part of the wall of the passage way.

George's knowledge of the area:

He has worked for people including next door neighbours of the deceased woman. From that it can be inferred he had a knowledge of the gardens at the rear of No. 3, Clifton Street and the two adjoining house.

And much was made of George standing for a considerable time opposite Miss Thomas's house on the evening:

Putting the evidence at its lowest value, it clearly indicates that during the very important fifteen minutes when the old lady was attacked the accused man had at least an opportunity of going into the house at the time.

Mr Jones stated the accused was interviewed by the police on three occasions; he said that the difficulties of interviewing a deaf and dumb person would be demonstrated. The interviews were conducted through two interpreters, the first on 13 January taking the form of question and answer, with the questions by the police being interpreted to the accused and his replies interpreted back. Mr Jones added that the defence might query the admissibility of these statements:

On January 18th, two police officers saw the accused at Laugharne police station. He indicated to them that he wanted to say something. They gave him a piece of paper, an exhibit in the case, and Roberts drew a house, which could clearly be identified as the house of the deceased old lady. He then drew two houses adjoining the cottage. The officers who were present when the house was drawn will indicate to you how the accused put across what he wanted to explain to them from the plan he had drawn. Following this there was a fresh interview with Roberts in the form of question and answer.

He then addressed the magistrates: 'If you are satisfied that there is a case that this man has to answer then I will ask you to commit the accused to stand his trial at the assizes.' However, before calling the evidence, Mr Thomas Crellin was sworn as a deaf and dumb interpreter. The prosecution concluded by saying, 'We are faced with a most unusual case and one of extreme difficulty because of the disability of the accused.'

At this point, Mr Myer Cohen for the defence said:

I think it is only right that I should say that from the observations of the defendant and upon the advice given to me by people who know him that it is believed to be impossible for any interpreter to interpret to this man anything but the most elementary phrases.

He went on:

In the event of his going for trial it may well be that a certain plea will be put forward at the assizes. So that it may not be said against the defence that no objection was made in the lower court, I request a note be taken that it is impossible for the evidence to be interpreted to the defendant. But to facilitate the hearing of the case now I do not make any objection to the procedure of interpreting at this stage.

Witnesses gave evidence on the finding of Miss Thomas, but when Mr Crellin, the interpreter, was handed the depositions of the first witness (Mr Jones) and started to interpret what had been said, George shook his head and waved his arms.

The interpreter exclaimed, 'It is simply useless trying to put this evidence to him, He says he does not know the witness and in order to interpret the address to him he would have to be taken there.'

No attempt was then made to transmit the evidence to George.

Further evidence was taken from the men who had found Miss Thomas and the doctor who suggested hospital, and the receiving doctor at the hospital.

George just shook his head.

Little was sought in cross-examination by the defence, save for the hospital doctor who agreed it was usual to find abrasions on manual workers (handymen).

George's movements and activities were traced through that afternoon. Mr Langdon described the purchase of the batteries and in cross-examination said that that he had always known George as a decent fellow and never known him to lose his temper. He lived, he said, in a world of his own. The only way he could be made to understand was by simple signs. Mr Langdon then demonstrated how simple the signs had to be.

Miss Lewis, a casual 'employer', felt he was completely trustworthy. Mr and Mrs

Phillips, however, could outline his standing outside of the house next to their shop. Mr Jenkins worked closely with George and he too demonstrated how 'simple' the signs he understood had to be. But what was interesting about Mr Jenkins' evidence was a man he saw later at just around 6.15 p.m.:

> I opened the garage door ... [and] ... I saw a man coming from near Miss Thomas's cottage ... the man was coming across the street towards me. Seeing me he veered off. I said 'good evening' to him, but he made no reply and pulled up the collar of his coat ... did not seem to have any headgear at all.

All witnesses described George as wearing a light cap that afternoon and evening. Mrs Lewis saw George at about 6.30 p.m. with a cap and he did not try to 'hide' himself. Miss Davies, who lived next door to Miss Thomas, said that George had worked for her in her garden up until three years before. DSupt Spooner had mentioned this but not the time lapse since this arrangement ceased. He also mentioned George had worked for another of Miss Thomas's neighbours, Mr Williams: he told the court George had *once* dug his garden. So with the missing cap and the *actual* facts of George's known presence in the vicinity of Miss Thomas's garden one begins to wonder what other 'facts' had been, could one say, 're-focused'?

Miss Vaughan said George had worked for her for thirty-three years:

> I conversed with him by simple signs and gestures. I did not find it difficult to tell him what jobs were needed to be done. His needs were very simple, and as far as I knew all he used his money for was to buy cigarettes and comic papers. He never seemed to bother about money.

Miss Vaughn went on to say that she was in court when George was brought up on remand. A woman acted as interpreter, and Miss Vaughn felt that with her knowledge of George and communications, she did not think he could understand what was being put to him.

DS Jones said that with Mrs Davies acting as interpreter, the accused said:

> I was walking along Clifton Street at 4 o'clock and went as far as the church. I came back about quarter past four. I saw Miss Thomas on the doorstep and saluted her. She is my friend. I did not speak to her, only saluted her as I passed I then walked home and had food. There was another man with me on the road when I went home. I was home about 5 o'clock and did not go out again.

To the layman this would seem to need quite a complex series of sign language movements. But would George be able to do this? He could communicate on a basic level. But because of his difficulties, training in sign language – that is to say the accepted alphabet and so forth – had not been taught him. It begs the question, did he actually 'say' this or did he say something else? For that matter did he understand what Mrs Davies asked him on DS Jones' behalf? But there was more to this 'questioning'.

'You were seen near Miss Thomas's house at half past five and at quarter passed [*sic*] six. Have you anything to say to that?'

George was said to reply: 'No. I was not there. I had had my food and stayed in the house reading.'

DS Jones said that Mrs Davies was told to ask the accused whether he understood, and the reply by Mrs Davies was: 'He has told me he understands and that it is true.'

DSupt Spooner saw George on 13 January, Mrs Davies was again interpreter but with her colleague (actually her husband who was deaf – and carried that awful label of 'dumb'). This interview was question-and-answer based, but in the course of the interview when George had been asked a question through Mrs Davies and shown a pen knife, he pointed to an injury below his knee. DSupt Spooner was asked, 'Were you satisfied that he understood the questions you were putting to him?' DSupt Spooner replied, 'My opinion was that he fully understood every question and gave a ready, intelligent answer.'

'He was shown a pen-knife and pointed to an injury below his knee...' I would love to know what George 'understood' to be the question and how when he 'pointed to an injury below his knee' this was an 'intelligent answer'. It does not seem that he was asked, so just what was George's understanding of the question in relation to the pen-knife?

On Sunday 18 January, George came to the police station at Laugharne. DSupt Spooner saw him with DS Millen:

> He made signs that he wanted to say something. I gestured the outline of a woman. He nodded. I then produced to him two photographs in an album of photographs of Clifton Street. Roberts pointed at Miss Thomas's house and nodded. He then made a sign that he wanted to write something. He was given pencil and a sheet of paper by Sergt. Millen. The accused proceeded to draw a sketch. When he completed a house which was in the centre of five houses in the sketch, he stopped, put down his pencil, gestured a woman, bowed his head sadly and touched his eyes with his handkerchief. He then recommenced drawing ... drew a sketch of himself and again pointed out to the middle house, gestured a woman and made thrusting motions.

DSupt Spooner said he showed George a knife and he nodded. But what did his nodding actually mean? One wonders if George were to have drawn a man holding a stick or a man with a knife, then this might portray something.

In cross-examination DSupt Spooner was asked:

'You assumed that by nodding his head Roberts gave affirmative answers?'

'Yes.'

'Do you know anything about illiterate deaf and dumb mutes?'

'No.'

'Did you hear the evidence of people who had known him for thirty years or more?'

'No.'

'Many of these people have stated he could only understand the most simple signs – people who have known him twenty and thirty years. You had never seen him before?'

'No.'

'You know nothing about the deaf and dumb language; nothing about illiterate deaf and dumb mutes, yet you say in your opinion that he fully understood every question?'

'Yes.'

'He gave, as you say ready, intelligent answers by nodding his head?'

'No.'

'By making signs?'

'Yes. I based my appraisement on the interrogation as a whole.'

PC Bennett did have some knowledge and had acted as interpreter during some of the police interviews. At the request of the defence, he put a question to George by signs. George was thought to be interested in PC Bennett's movements and nodded his head several times. After the test, PC Bennett said in his opinion George had understood the questions put to him. But what were the questions?

Mrs Davies gave evidence: for nineteen years she had acted as court interpreter, and she had been interview interpreter between the police and George. Mrs Davies said George understood crude signs typical of the rural area, lip reading and some 'plus' mime. On 13 January, and again on 18 January, she was present when George was interviewed by DSupt Spooner.

In cross-examination Mr Cohen asked:

'Would I be right in saying that there are no recognised standard signs universally employed by deaf persons?'

'No. there are not. They vary In England and Wales, France and America [*sic*]'.

'Nodding the head is not to be taken as signifying comprehension?'

'Nodding the head downwards would be.'

'Would you agree that a person having contact with the accused over many years would be able to "converse" with him better than somebody who has just met him?'

'We had no difficulty with this man.'

'That is not an answer to my question.'

Mr Cohen suggested people who knew George well would 'know his peculiarities'. He also suggested that the question asked by PC Bennett should be shared with the court but this was refused by the magistrates.

It has to be said that sign language had to evolve rather than the whole alphabet and language suddenly becoming known one day. So it would have started simply and grown – in this century it is not unusual to see people 'signing', so its growth has been helped and enhanced. But for George Roberts in the middle of the last century it relied on much patience from his friends, and Miss Watkins was a good case in point. She said she had been able to 'converse' with George by getting to know the simple signs she had learnt from him over many years. Mr Cohen asked:

> 'You have known him a long time. Do you think a person who had never seen Roberts before could understand him and get messages over to him?'
> 'Not very easily.'

Dr Freezer, the pathologist, described Miss Thomas's fractured skull:

> Miss Thomas had a fracture of the skull on the right side, splitting the roof of the right eye socket and breaking the side of the skull above the right eye into fragments. The fractures of the right fore-arm occurred at about the same time as the other injuries. There were two wounds in the chest which perforated the chest wall, one having pricked the lung.

Emlyn Davies, of the Home Office Forensic Science Laboratory, Cardiff, said on 11 January he went to George's house and took some clothing including a mackintosh. At Miss Thomas's cottage he took a stick, a broom and a sample of plaster from the hall. He received a sample of hair of Miss Thomas. At one end of the stick he found four bloodstains and associated with one of the stains were human hairs, which were firmly caught in the wood. These hairs were similar to Miss Thomas's hair. It was clear the stick had been used to beat Miss Thomas.

Cross-examined, Mr Davies said he did not take a sample of plaster from George's house. Colin Tibbitt, of the Forensic Science Laboratory, said he took a patch of green paint or distemper from the back of George's coat. George Carter, of the Forensic Science Laboratory, said the green distemper taken from the mackintosh resembled in colour and ingredients the green distemper taken from the cottage. The white material also found on the coat differed from the white material in the sample of plaster. Cross-examined, Mr Carter said the green distemper was the ordinary commercial type of distemper which could be purchased in any stores.

So the prosecution had some difficulty in proving George had been at the scene of the crime.

Mr Cohen for the defence said there was no case to answer; he said it was a case of mass contradictions. A large number of witnesses who had known George for years had said that with his limited power of communication, he could only understand the simplest of signs, and only by similar means could he get over to people what he was trying to say.

Mr Cohen suggested:

You have complete strangers who have come into court to say that they knew better than all these people who had known Roberts for years. Detective-Superintendent Spooner, of Scotland Yard, who had seen Roberts for the first time on January 12th, tells you that he was satisfied that this man knew what was being said and was able to give a coherent answer. How far have these police witnesses been guessing what they thought Roberts was saying?

And Mr Cohen continued his submission by asserting that;

a test to demonstrate a police officer's ability to put certain questions to accused [*sic*] would have enabled the magistrates to judge how far they could accept statements alleged to have been made by the accused and which had been produced as exhibits.

However, the test was refused, though one had taken place, the result of which was not admissible.

Finally, and working backwards, Mr Cohen discussed the witness statement of George's movements:

Is the prosecution trying to fix this crime on to a man seen in the vicinity? It is admitted that Roberts did not hide himself afterwards. If anyone is going out to do anything wrong, is he going to stand in the main street of Laugharne afterwards to be seen by anyone. Is he the type of man who witnesses have never known to lose his temper, to have killed a woman and then a few seconds later walk casually away along the road?

As for the light going out in Miss Thomas's house, 'was there someone there who could hear and then put the light out?'

The magistrates felt there was a *prima facie* (on the face of it) case for trial and George Roberts was sent for trial at Carmarthenshire Assizes.

It is not surprising this turn of events came about because magistrates are not qualified and are advised in court as to the best course to take. This was a murder and so, for justice to be seen to be done, it should go to an Assize Court.

There were two issues facing the court:

The first was a 'fitness to plead' issue, which under normal circumstances should be dealt with first, if the defendant is suffering from 'insanity'. I am discussing 1953 Mental Health terminology, which changed radically in the 1959 and 1983 Mental Health Acts. At the time the crime is committed then he may not be responsible for his actions as he did not know that what he did was wrong. Therefore, 'intent' or 'wilful' did not apply. He would be taken to a place where, security acknowledged and the public protected, he could be treated. As such, he would not serve a sentence but would be detained during His/Her Majesty's pleasure. Now he would be detained, perhaps in hospital, but 'without limit of time' ('routine' patients, detained for assessment or treatment, had a time limit).

But all of this relies on a mental health assessment being possible. In George's case it was not.

The second issue is a general issue – guilt or non-guilt of the crime. A jury could be sworn to try the 'fitness to plead' issue, but with no possibility of having evidence on which to decide whether he is sane or insane. This left the general issue of murder. But to say it 'left' the general issue of murder is not quite right, rather it sidestepped it.

The dilemma was whether George could be held in a secure institution, probably for the rest of his life as a criminal lunatic, when he may be neither a criminal nor a lunatic? But also this would mean that little or no further police investigation of the crime would be made.

Helping things along, of course, was the defence, who had submitted that there was no case to answer. Complicating matters was the magistrates saying there was.

A unique legal brain was needed.

The case opened at Carmarthen Assizes on 6 March 1953, Mr Justice Patrick Devlin presided. Mr Jones-Roberts acted for the prosecution, and George was represented by Mr Harvard Evans.

When the Clerk of Assizes called on the accused to plead, George made no reply. Mr Jones-Roberts, for the prosecution, said that the two questions the jury had to consider were, firstly, whether George was mute of malice or by visitation of God; and, secondly, whether he was fit to plead to the indictment.

Mr Phillips told the court he had known George for twenty-nine years and, in that time, he had neither heard him speak nor respond to any sound. The jury found he was 'mute by visitation of God'.

Then the question of George's fitness to plead was discussed, Mr Justice Devlin addressed the defence: 'I wish to make it quite clear whether you are satisfied that on the evidence in the lower court the prosecution can make out a prima facie case against the accused.' Mr Harvard Evans stated, 'My view of the evidence is that there is no prima facie case.'

However, as the law stood, if there was no *prima facie* case and George was declared unfit to plead, then the only order the court could make, and by statute, was that George should be detained. Mr Evans said he found this 'distressing'.

He added:

> Whatever statements are in the depositions in this case must be excluded because the person is not fit to communicate. One is left with the other evidence on the depositions. Having read most carefully these depositions I submit that there is no prima facie case.

So this was the basis of the legal argument that was at the centre of the case, the statements that were in the depositions, or could the evidence of George's 'confession' and what he was alleged to have communicated to the police through an interpreter be admitted? If the evidence was deemed inadmissible, the prosecution may have to review their case.

Mr Justice Devlin asked Mr Harvard Evans for the defence:

> 'You take the view that the prima facie case is not made out on the depositions, or on such part of the depositions that are admissible. Therefore, you take the view that the prosecution cannot prove their case.'
> 'I say that definitely.'
> 'It seems to me quite wrong that we should take the course necessary in the indictment that a man be detained indefinitely when he might be innocent.'

Simply put, there was no case.

The test of guilty or not guilty was to prove as problematic as sane or insane. The one course available would hinge on whether or not the prosecution could prove their case, in which case the law would prescribe guilty but insane. Mr Justice Devlin wondered if there was anything wrong with the defence pleading to the general issue – i.e., guilty or not guilty of the charge and asking the jury to deliver a verdict of not guilty.

The defence thought they were almost obliged to take this course, but Mr Justice Devlin said he would be very reluctant to accept a plea of unfit to plead (i.e. sane or insane) and make an order incarcerating what might well be an innocent man.

Therefore the case was deferred and the jury discharged.

The case went to Glamorganshire Assizes in Cardiff and was heard on 23 and 24 March 1953. Here, George was represented by Mr Edmund Davies QC and Mr Vincent Lloyd-Jones QC acted for the prosecution.

When the case was opened, the counsels for the prosecution, defence and Mr Justice Devlin discussed (legal argument) George's fitness to plead. The case was unique, asserted Mr Edmund Davies, but he had raised an objection to the admission of some evidence which were the statements George allegedly made to the police through the interpreter.

Mr Justice Devlin stated, 'This is a case which, apart from these statements, is very slender indeed. So slender, that it is hardly worth considering and it seems to me that the position of the prosecution is a rather doubtful one.'

When Mr Justice Devlin had the jury sworn, he told the jury:

When a person cannot answer to his name, the first question is whether he is silent by malice or mute by visitation of God. That is the first issue which you have been sworn to try. Evidence is before you which is unchallenged.

This jury, as the previous one, found George mute by visitation of God. But was he sane or insane, guilty or not guilty? Two separate issues, but was Mr Justice Devlin proposing a unique course for a unique case – that is to say deciding the two issues together? An answer had to be found to both, but which first? He said, 'It has got to be investigated. The only question is, at what stage.'

There was no authority, he added, that prevented counsel for the defence, who wanted to test the prosecution's case, from having the right to do so and at the same time establishing whether the accused person was one who could be communicated with. So by looking at the general issue, (guilt or non-guilt) then the answer to the question of fitness to plead (sane or insane) would simultaneously be answered. He added:

> To insist upon this issue of fitness being tried might result in the detention of a man as a criminal lunatic when he is in fact innocent. The investigations which might result in the apprehension of the true criminal would not then take place.

He then said that he would not swear the jury to try separately the fitness to plead issue, but would swear them to try the general issue of murder. The jury then returned to court and were sworn in to try George on the murder charge.

Mr Lloyd-Jones prepared to open for the prosecution, and Mr Justice Devlin asked:

> 'Is it right that apart from the statement alleged to have been made by him, the only evidence to connect Roberts with the crime is that about half-an-hour before the probable time of the crime he was seen observing the house?'
>
> 'Yes.'
>
> 'After that time he was seen walking away from the churchyard and some unidentified man was seen walking away from a waste piece of ground. You propose to strengthen it by producing statements from a man with whom there is no certain means of communication.'

The time to question the admissibility of George's confession was nigh! But it was a dilemma because the charge had been brought, and Mr Justice Devlin had to follow the strict path of the law. He asked:

> 'If I should rule that these statements should not go to the jury is there any evidence on which a jury might convict?'
>
> 'I think not, my lord.'

Mr Justice Devlin said he thought it was impossible. He invited the prosecution to call their evidence relating to the alleged statements before any other evidence. Moreover, when Superintendent Jones gave his evidence of visiting George at his home and could only communicate with him through his uncle, Mr Edmund Davies for the defence suggested this was hearsay.

The judge ruled that any questions put through the uncle could not be given in evidence, and Superintendent Jones then went on to give evidence of a later date, when he interviewed George in the presence of the interpreters, Mr and Mrs Davies. Mr Edmund Davies said that he objected to anything at this stage unless an interpreter was first called.

Mrs Beddoe-Davies was sworn. Mr Justice Devlin asked: 'You say you made him understand perfectly?'

'Yes.'

Mr Edmund Davies: 'There are a number of questions I wish to put to her before she says what is alleged to have taken place.'

The jury left while legal arguments took place on the admissibility of this part of the evidence: the so-called confessions of George, which were understood by the police and Mrs Davies perfectly, although the villagers all said George could only understand the most basic communications. Were the depositions of the police, *vis-à-vis* George's confession, reliable?

After hearing legal argument for both sides, Mr Justice Devlin ruled the evidence inadmissible. Therefore, the prosecution's case was that George:

1. Was seen opposite Miss Thomas's house.
2. Was later seen walking away from the house.
3. And a month or so previous he had been seen with a knife.

These three issues dictated that on the general issue (guilt or non-guilt), guilt could not be proved: George was innocent. The prosecution announced that 'in all the circumstances ... the right course ... to adopt ... is not to proceed with the case and offer no further evidence.'

Mr Justice Devlin directed the jury to return a verdict of 'not guilty'.

The case remains unsolved.

ANNIE LOUISE KEMPSON, OXFORD, 1931

Part 1

Henry Daniel Seymour is the name recorded as that of the man who murdered Annie Louisa Kempson in Oxford on the morning of Saturday 1 August 1931, for which he was tried, found guilty and hanged. Whether the name on his birth certificate was the same as the name on his death certificate is doubtful. And whether the name on his marriage certificate was the same as the name on his birth certificate is, again, doubtful. He also had a number of assumed names, and a long list of convictions, both in the UK and abroad. Only one of his convictions was for violence and was serious enough to warrant a custodial sentence, which in the event was not given. But it is doubtful that he was guilty of the murder, and, as I will show, the evidence against him was circumstantial. There were no eyewitnesses, his presence could not be proved at the scene of the crime; there is no certainty as to exactly when the murder took place, and a considerable number of witnesses said they saw Mrs Kempson on the afternoon of Saturday 1 August 1931.

Henry Seymour was described as a cabinet maker, aged thirty-nine, but for some years he had been employed as a commercial traveller. According to his criminal record, he was born in Birmingham in 1873, but according to birth record he was not, at any rate not as Henry Daniel Seymour. It is likely his age would have been nearer to late fifties than late thirties. Where he grew up is a mystery, and his past varied, sometimes he was a doctor's son born in London and at other times he said he was born in Birmingham. One story was that he left England and went to South Africa in around 1906 where he led a life of criminal activity, and later imprisonment.

He was back in England by 1920 as he was charged with housebreaking; it was the Metropolitan Police who investigated, and his convictions in South Africa were verified by fingerprints and photographs. In 1923, he was sentenced to five years' imprisonment following conviction for the theft of jewellery from a house where he was employed as a cook.

By 1930, Henry was out of prison and living in Devon, selling vacuum cleaners manufactured by the Tellus Company. In July 1930, he was convicted of making what was described as a 'murderous assault' on a woman to whom he sold a vacuum cleaner. Strangely he was only 'bound over' for this offence and ordered to pay the victim some compensation, but he never did.

He had worked for the Tellus Company for about two years and later had covered the Oxford and Aylesbury districts, but this had not been without further criminal activity. He went to work for a company selling ladies' clothing, Yarnstrong's, but channelled a considerable sum of money (over £90, which would now be the equivalent of about £5,000) into his own possession. Henry was said to have then dodged about between Aylesbury, Folkestone and Brighton as he feared his arrest.

He was finally arrested in Brighton where he had taken the lease on a flat in the name of Mr Harvey. He had also used the names Henderson, Henry David Goodchild and Harry Johnson. He was married and his wife remained in Oxford together with their son.

Annie Louisa Reynolds had become Mrs William Kempson in the late summer of 1905. Mr Kempson ran a fruiterer's shop in St Clements Street, which is over towards Headington on the eastern side of Oxford. He was just about twenty years older than his wife and the marriage bore no children. Mr Kempson died in the mid-1920s, which actually left Mrs Kempson quite comfortably off – she owned some business as well as residential property which provided her with an income. She was by now fifty-eight years of age.

Mrs Kempson lived in Boundary House in St Clements Street, a pleasant three-bedroom semi-detached house. There was a front sitting room and what was described as a rear parlour together with a kitchen at the rear of the property. She had a lodger, Miss Eleanor Jane Williams, who had been with her for about six years, and who worked as a waitress in a café in the centre of Oxford.

It was on 1 August that both women had arranged to go away on holiday, but not together. They had breakfast as usual and Miss Williams left for work at around 9.20 a.m. Mrs Kempson was having a cup of tea when Miss Williams left and, apart from being seen admitting a man to her house at about 10.00 a.m., it was claimed she was not seen alive again – a major issue which I will look at presently.

Mrs Kempson was due to leave Oxford the next afternoon and travel to Highgate to visit a friend. When she failed to arrive, her friend contacted Mrs Kempson's brother, who also lived in Oxford, and he went to her house. However, he did nothing then, save for sending a telegram to a friend, but over the weekend fears for Mrs Kempson's safety mounted. Her brother, together with his son, gained entry to Mrs Kempson's house at around 7.30 p.m. on the following Monday, and they found Mrs Kempson lying dead on the floor of the back parlour. She lay on her back and her head was neatly covered up with pillows and a rough hair doormat. Mrs Kempson had been struck on the back of her head, on the forehead, and on the right side of the head. The last two blows had fractured her skull and had evidently been made by a round, blunt instrument such as a hammer. She had also been stabbed with a sharp cutting instrument on the right side of her neck, and this severed her carotid artery.

Suspicion was directed toward Henry when a trade card bearing his name was found on Mrs Kempson's mantlepiece; there was also a receipt from 'H. S.' on behalf of the Yarnstrong Company, from whom he had embezzled about £90. It was for this he was eventually arrested, and was then interviewed by the police in connection with the murder of Mrs Kempson.

Henry's movements on the morning of 1 August were scrutinised, and unless Mrs Kempson was murdered at some time between 9.45 a.m. and 11.00 a.m. on that Saturday morning, she could not have been murdered by Henry Seymour.

So the two issues at the core of the case were:

1. Was Mrs Kempson murdered between these hours on that Saturday morning?
2. What evidence was there that Henry Seymour murdered her?

It was claimed that the evidence that Mrs Kempson was killed between 9.45 a.m. and 11.00 a.m. on Saturday 1 August was 'overwhelming', so this needs to be discussed. However, briefly, Miss Williams said Mrs Kempson had tomatoes for supper the night before – Friday 31 July – and Sir Bernard Spilsbury, the noted pathologist, could confirm Mrs Kempson did eat tomatoes about twelve hours before her death, but there was nothing conclusive about when she ate the tomatoes. If they were the tomatoes the remains of which Miss Williams saw, then it would date the crime as 1 August, but if she had a supper including tomatoes on the Saturday night, then it paves the way for a Sunday 2 August death. Sir Bernard also said there was bread, butter and custard in the intestines, which had been consumed about an hour or two before death, but this does not prove the food was consumed on the Saturday morning.

Mrs Kempson was known to be a lady whose habits and routines were methodical. Her usual routine was that after Miss Williams left for work each morning she would have her own breakfast and then go upstairs to tidy and make the beds before she removed her hair curlers, which she usually slept in. After this, she would tidy the front of the house by sweeping the front doorstep and garden. When her body was discovered, Mrs Kempson still wore her hair curlers and the beds were unmade.

The newspapers delivered on the Sunday and Monday morning had been found folded under the door just as they had been delivered. It had been about five years since Mr Kempson had died and so her usual routine for a Saturday afternoon was to attend his grave, tidy it and place fresh flowers. However, she had not been there on that Saturday – the flowers were clearly old and from the previous week, and the grave had not been attended to. Furthermore she would often visit a shopkeeper (who was also her gardener) on her way home from the cemetery, but did not do so on that Saturday.

On Friday 31 July, Mrs Kempson had gone shopping with her friend and had bought a new pair of shoes. On the bus on the return from town, Mrs Kempson told her friend that she was to visit her brother, and so the friend took the shoes from her and arranged to bring them to her house on the Saturday, the following morning. Her friend, Mrs Ruth Steele, did attend the house at around 11.00 a.m., but the door was not answered. She thought Mrs Kempson must be out so she lifted the window adjacent to the front door and dropped the shoes onto a Chesterfield sofa in the front room; this is where they were found later by the police.

It was felt that the points above proved Mrs Kempson was murdered between 9.45 a.m. and 11.00 a.m., but there are strong arguments to question this. Moreover, there were a considerable number of people who said they saw Mrs Kempson on the afternoon of Saturday 1 August, but they were all said to have been mistaken! Some gave evidence in court and some did not. It may have been pure coincidence that those witnesses who did give evidence were considered to be mistaken, but others who said in statements that they had seen Mrs Kempson were not called to court;so effectively their evidence was suppressed, or at any rate the jury did not hear what they had to say.

So what evidence was there that Henry Seymour was guilty of this murder? He freely admitted he was in Oxford that day, and said he wanted to see his wife though the fear of arrest for the money he had embezzled from Yarnstrong's was a strong motive for not going to his wife.

Henry purchased a hammer and a screwdriver from an ironmongers – Fulkes – on the afternoon of 31 July. He was found in possession of this hammer (Mrs Kempson sustained three blows to her head and was stabbed through the neck by a sharp implement). Henry said he bought these implements in the afternoon but it was said to have been proved he actually bought a wood chisel and a hammer at, or just after, 8.00 p.m. that night. Whether this was proved or not again needs some discussion.

There can be no doubt that Henry was a conman and when he spoke he often departed from the truth, but whether he was a murderer is another question. But he did know a number of people in the Oxford area. A Mrs Alice Andrews lent him some money on the evening of 31 July, but as he missed his bus to Aylesbury she gave him a night's accommodation – she took in occasional bed and breakfast guests. One commentator claimed that Mrs Andrews owed her life to the fact that her son was also in the house that night – this could be said to give some indication of the conjecture in the press which was rife, and may have clogged the thought processes of the jury.

On Saturday 1 August, the suggested day of the murder, Henry left Mrs Andrews' at around 9.30 a.m. and Mrs Andrews' house was only a few hundred yards from Mrs Kempson's. Mrs Andrews later reported seeing some paper parcels he had which contained tools he had purchased – and Mrs Andrews was to be solid in her evidence that it was a hammer and a ¾-inch bladed wood chisel that she saw. Mrs Andrews' son, it was claimed, had also seen the wood chisel.

At just a few minutes to 10.00 a.m., a man who knew Mrs Kempson, but only by sight, was passing her house just as she admitted a man who answered Henry's description, but he was only seen from the back so just what part of the description matched Henry is open to question. And there was no mention of an identity parade later. But apparently Mrs Kempson opened the door, the gentleman seemed to bow and then entered the house – interestingly this gentleman is referred to as 'the prisoner' in the records.

But it was Henry who was seen by a Mrs Florence Collins a little later at a bus stop, which was a few hundred yards from Mrs Kempson's house. Mrs Collins knew Henry quite well. This was timed at just around 11.00 a.m., or possibly a little later. She said he was nervous and agitated.

However, at his trial he gave what was described as an 'entirely unconvincing and incredible account of how he spent his time from 9.30 a.m. when he left Mrs. Andrews' house carrying the hammer and chisel, and 11.00 a.m. when he was seen by Mrs. Collins at the bus stop'.

The motive of the murder was evidently robbery because it was reported there were several purses and wallets open and empty in the sitting room, and the bedrooms upstairs had been ransacked. It was also offered to the jury that Mrs Kempson had purchased a Tellus vacuum cleaner from Henry and had given him five pounds as a deposit. Five pounds was then a considerable sum to have in the house.

Henry said that after he had spoken to Mrs Collins at the bus stop, he walked to the town of Wheatley, which would have taken him about an hour, and it was here that he boarded a bus for Aylesbury.

The hotel in Aylesbury where he was staying were keen to see some money from their guest but he managed to move his luggage to the Greyhound Hotel before he left the area to go to Brighton where he had rented a flat, it was here that he was arrested on 15 August.

In the flat in Brighton, life for Henry was anything but straightforward. It was a flat of three rooms, and through the floor of one of his rooms, which was immediately above the landlady's sitting room, two holes had been bored. It was suggested these boreholes were made with a chisel, but the chisel Mrs Andrews had seen was never found; Henry said he had not purchased a chisel anyway, it was a screwdriver. But these bore holes enabled Henry, so it was argued, to have a complete view of Mrs Belmore's sitting room and also to hear anything that was said there.

The police recovered Henry's suitcase from the Greyhound Hotel and found the hammer and various other tools. The label had been removed, as had the firm's private mark, from the hammer.

What was relevant of course was the pathologist's report of the injuries, the cause of death and the time of death of Mrs Kempson. Briefly, he said the wounds on the head of the deceased and the head of the hammer were of a differing size, so it was suggested a rug was held over her head to account for the larger-sized wounds from the smaller-sized hammer, but there is no evidence of a struggle in the room in which the murder appears to have happened. Again, a more detailed discussion is needed.

The Chief Constable of Oxford asked for the assistance of Scotland Yard so it would be useful to consider the senior detective's findings. There was also the quite bizarre recording by a DS of the judge's summing up, and in shorthand, so what tales this document will tell would be worth analysis; but one should also consider what tales this document does not tell.

Part 2

By the Monday after the murder, the Chief Constable of Oxford Constabulary, Mr Charles Fox, contacted the Metropolitan Police at Scotland Yard to request their assistance. It was at about a quarter to ten that morning that Chief Detective Inspector (now referred to as Detective Chief Inspector) John Horwell heard of the crime and was given the task of investigating and to bring those responsible to book. After receiving instructions and briefing assistants, he contacted Mr Fox in Oxford.

DCI Horwell also made contact, at Mr Fox's request, with the Home Office pathologist, Sir Bernard Spilsbury, to seek his assistance and to perform the post-mortem examination. Sir Bernard made arrangements to travel to Oxford on the Tuesday afternoon. At around lunchtime on Tuesday 4 August, the police officers from Scotland Yard left Paddington Station in London bound for Oxford where they arrived at around 2.00 p.m. Mr Fox was at the station to meet them. He explained that Mrs Kempson's body had been discovered at around 7.30 p.m. the previous evening. DCI Horwell was taken to the house where he was shown the murder scene with Mrs Kempson's body still in the position in which it had been found. He noted that she was lying on her back on the floor, the floor being carpeted, but there was a 'fluffy doormat' covering the upper part of Mrs Kempson's body. Her legs were pointed straight out and no thoughts were expressed of any sexual motive. Her clothing was actually reported to be quite tidy although her hair was still in curlers. DCI Horwell noted the jewellery Mrs Kempson wore: a wrist watch, her wedding ring and also a broach. She was dressed in what was described as a black 'working frock' with a cotton overall, black stockings and shoes. There was no sign of a struggle and DCI Horwell reported that nothing likely to be the murder weapon was found in the house.

As well as the doormat covering part of the body, there was also an arrangement of three cushions covering her head and shoulders. There was no suggestion this arrangement was symbolic. DCI Horwell thought the fluffy doormat had been taken from the hall-side of the front sitting room door. There was a fairly large pool of blood which was still moist and reached from her head towards the corner of the room, just over four feet away. No splashes or spots of blood were found on the floor, walls or furniture of the room. Close searching failed to find any blood in any other rooms of the house.

There were no signs of a forcible entry to the house, all doors and windows were examined. The body had been found when Mrs Kempson's nephew and his father (Mrs Kempson's brother) had got into the house through a back bedroom window. A window was found unlocked in the front of the house though this was pulled down shut.

It was thought that some of the pieces of furniture in a cluttered back sitting room may have borne fingerprints, but the only identifiable mark was Mrs Kempson's. In Miss Williams' room, there was some evidence to suggest the person responsible had been wearing gloves.

In DCI Horwell's report, he described the house as being of an 'old-fashioned' design, but it was only about twenty-five or thirty years old as it was semi-detached. The front garden was surrounded by railings and had an iron gate; the front garden occupied about fourteen feet between the pavement and the house, and anyone passing by would have quite a clear view of the whole of the front of the house. There was a side gate leading to the rear of the house, but this was usually padlocked. The back garden was large and thickly planted with trees and shrubs. Although Mrs Kempson had a gardener, the garden was overgrown. There were two sheds that were close to the back door and another shed down at the bottom of the garden.

The staircase to the first floor led up from the hall. All of the rooms downstairs and up were described as overly furnished. The back parlour had double-glazed doors that led out into the back garden, but the light was cut off a little by the rear of the neighbouring house. There was also a dividing wall between Mrs Kempson's house and her neighbour's, which belonged to her neighbour. The next house did not overlook any part of Mrs Kempson's house.

DCI Horwell described the back parlour as small and heavily furnished, and the space between a small table and the sideboard, where the body was found, was only 2ft 6ins. Sir Bernard could make an examination of the body where it was found. It was thought the wounds on the head had been caused by some form of blunt instrument, and a hammer seemed likely. Two of the blows had actually penetrated the skull, and the wound in the neck appeared more like a stab wound that was about 2½ inches below the right ear; it seemed likely this latter wound had been inflicted by a sharp instrument. Two small abrasions were seen: one on the back of Mrs Kempson's neck and one behind the left ear. It seemed as though she had been struck from behind, which may have stunned her, and the possibility was that the other wounds had been inflicted after she had fallen to the floor.

There was nothing to indicate that she had been attacked elsewhere and dragged to where she was found, as the room was undisturbed and there was not a trail of blood. Sir Bernard noted some small spots of blood on the front of the sideboard, level with Mrs Kempson's head, which were possibly due to her coughing before her death. It was thought the wound in her neck, which had severed her carotid artery and pierced her mouth, would have resulted in blood draining through the mouth and throat rather than externally. It was also suggested that the cushions under which she was covered had been placed after the attack. Blood marks were found on one of the cushions but it was likely this was where the sharp cutting weapon had been wiped after the attack.

The whole of the house and the scene of the murder were photographed.

Small pieces of jewellery were found around the house, which suggested that if the motive for the crime was robbery then money appeared to be the main target. The back parlour, scene of the murder, Mrs Kempson's and Miss Williams' bedrooms had also been ransacked. There were a variety of handbags and purses, all of which had been opened and emptied, in the back parlour.

Part 3

Both the ladies were due to depart for a holiday and, after breakfast at around 9.30 a.m. on the Saturday, Miss Williams paid Mrs Kempson her weekly rent of 11/- of which Mrs Kempson gave her 1/- back. She left to go to work first and intended to catch her bus for Chipping Norton after she finished work that afternoon. Mrs Kempson's suitcase was found in the bedroom fully packed and ready to go; her return coach ticket to London was also found, unused, dated Sunday 2 August.

It was estimated that the minimum amount of cash in her possession was £2 or £3, which may have included the 10/- (note) paid in rent by Miss Williams and this money had most likely been in one of the purses or handbags.

Mrs Kempson owned several houses and a shop from which she drew rents, but it is unlikely she would have had a great deal of cash from this around the house. And the rents were usually collected on her behalf by her brother who would also bank the money.

It was argued that the lodger, Miss Williams, was the last person to see Mrs Kempson alive, which is an issue to discuss later. But just to follow DCI Horwell's train of thought for a while, this would have been at around 9.30 a.m. on the Saturday 1 August. This was when she left for work, after which she was to travel on her holidays directly from her place of employment in the city centre. DCI Horwell built his theory as to the time of Mrs Kempson's death from this; he said he found several things which (strongly) indicated she had been killed at some time before midday on the Saturday: the breakfast things had not been washed, beds not made, no sign of a midday meal or preparation of, and Sunday's and Monday's newspapers were found just below the letterbox as delivered.

It may well be that these issues did 'strongly' indicate that Mrs Kempson had been killed at some time before midday on the Saturday, but there is room for doubt. It is known that she had a visitor after Miss Williams' departure on the Saturday morning, this may have delayed Mrs Kempson from washing up the breakfast things because a) he murdered her shortly afterwards or b) what they found were the Sunday morning breakfast things. The beds were not made – this possibly suggests the time of the murder, but was it that Miss Williams' bed had not been made as she was entertaining a guest and he had arrived as she prepared to do these chores? It is possible Mrs Kempson had not made the beds because if both she and Miss Williams were to go away, then she may have planned to make up the beds with clean bedding, or even stripped the beds of linen and left them to 'air'.

However, Mrs Kempson had a guest arrive at around 10.00 a.m. The guest was said to 'bow' when she answered the door and she admitted him to the house with little or no hesitation or conversation, which suggests it was someone she knew. So Mrs Kempson may have simply put off Miss Williams' bedroom chores until the following day. As for the man seen to enter the house – there was no identity parade recorded. DCI Horwell further asserts that no midday meal had been prepared, which could mean it had been prepared, eaten and washed up – but that no Sunday meal was prepared.

There is one thing in the details of Henry Seymour's life that begs attention – he was a criminal and probably this was his main occupation; selling vacuum cleaners and latterly ladies' attire was perhaps his legitimate foot in the door. It is possible that he would knock on someone's door in broad daylight, be admitted (he did know her), carry a hammer in one pocket and a chisel/screwdriver in another and wait until Mrs Kempson's back was turned before he bludgeoned her to death. That is what the jury seemed to think. But the hammer, found in his possession was, according to the pathologist, the wrong size; one suggestion was it was wrapped in the rug she was partly covered with. So did Mrs Kempson lead her 'guest' into the back parlour and pause momentarily while her assailant wrapped the hammer in the rug? If it was Henry, and Mrs Kempson had casually mentioned she was going on holiday the next day and that her lodger had already gone, then would Henry not have returned after dark and robbed her?

That is how a criminal would operate and there are a number of things to support this. Firstly, there was only one occasion when he had used violence and this was not proved to be connected to a crime he was committing. Secondly, he knew there would be 'rich pickings' in the house and the lodger was away. Thirdly, he was such a good locksmith he could actually design the keys for a mass breakout of a prison in South Africa in 1912, so a suburban semi would be easy – though he would be breaking in rather than out! Finally, he could enter the house and stealthily make his way up to Mrs Kempson's bedroom and, provided he could get to her before she could put on the light, could have blindfolded her, tied her up and taken his time to relieve her of as much booty as he wished. He was an intelligent man; mindless violence would not fit the picture. The key question here is could he get into the house, find his way upstairs, and have a good possibility of 'disabling' any possible raising of the alarm by Mrs Kempson's waking, switching on a light and screaming blue murder? He would need to know a small basic fact that he would have picked up from Mrs Kempson the moment he first met her: she was 'stone deaf'. It was noted in DCI Horwell's report that there was evidence that an intruder had got in and out previously – and on more than one occasion – with no visible signs of entry or exit over a five-month period up to February 1931.

What then of the newspapers that had been delivered, the Sunday and the Monday newspapers found just as they had dropped through the letterbox? There is another trait to Mrs Kempson which suggests that the 'facts', as DCI Horwell presented them, do not fit. She was going on holiday on the Sunday, so why was a newspaper delivered on the Monday? Those were the days before the pattern of the doormat was not permanently covered by junk mail and free newspapers, but Mrs Kempson has been described as 'very frugal' in her living, or as DCI Horwell put it 'tight with money' – would she not have cancelled her newspapers?

So it is not quite as clear-cut as DCI Horwell would have us believe just when Mrs Kempson met her end.

Part 4

There was an abundance of statements taken, not all of which were consistent with the known facts. This is to be expected, as after a day the memory fades and after two days even more so. If after three days one remembers something specific it would be because of a particular reason, but if not then there is the danger of confusing one day with another. So even if one gets the time correct, then one has to be sure it is the correct day.

But there are particular days of the week where things might stand out. For example, one working day might be the same as the next as far as routine goes, but the weekend days are different. And if now, in the twenty-first century, Saturday and Sunday are beginning to resemble each other – shops open, football, racing etc. – when in those days Sunday would still be a quiet and sedate time, and quite in contrast to the Saturday bustle.

So if someone in a job could single out Saturday then their memory could be quite sound. Mr James Horn was a house decorator but on Saturdays he would tend to his allotment. He lived in the street directly opposite to Mrs Kempson's house and as he walked up this street he came, as DCI Horwell described it, 'face to face' with her house. This was shortly after five minutes to ten. Mr Horn saw Mrs Kempson open her door to the man stood on her doorstep, and then she opened the door fully to let him in; no speech passed between Mrs Kempson and the guest, and this more than suggests he was someone she knew, and knew quite well. Mr Horn could describe the man as about 5ft 4ins tall and 'rather broad across the shoulders'. He described the man as wearing dark trousers and a dark coat – rather long and loose fitting – with a light coat over his left shoulder. Unfortunately, Mr Horn only saw the man from the back so to identify him would be difficult.

There was a public house on the corner opposite Mrs Kempson's house, the Duke of Edinburgh, and between 9.40 and 9.45 a.m., Miss Violet Reedes, who worked at the pub, was outside scrubbing the steps. She saw a man knocking at the door of Mrs Kempson's house but there was no answer, and the man walked away. She described the man as about 5 feet in height, and said he wore muddy fawn trousers and a blue coat, with a mackintosh over his left shoulder. But according to Miss Reedes he also wore a cap. She did not see his face but was sure she could recognise him again!

DCI Horwell felt that if Mrs Kempson was dead by 11.00 a.m. on the morning of 1 August then her attacker then ransacked the house for money. However, there was another caller that morning and although she did not gain entry to the house, DCI Horwell felt she disturbed the attacker, which explains why some of the jewellery and other money was untouched. This though is conjecture. However, the witness was someone who knew Mrs Kempson well enough to go shopping with her.

On the Friday evening, 31 July, Mrs Kempson knocked on the door of a friend of hers, Mrs Ruth Steele, with the suggestion the two women went shopping together. Mrs Kempson bought a new pair of shoes and they returned to Headington by bus; Mrs Kempson was planning to travel further to visit her brother, so when Mrs Steele got off the bus, she left Mrs Kempson on the bus. Mrs Steele took the shoes Mrs Kempson had bought with the arrangement that she would drop them off the following morning. At around 11.00 a.m., Mrs Steele knocked on Mrs Kempson's door and also held her finger on the bell for a good long time. There was no answer so Mrs Steele, who had noticed one of the front room windows was open at the bottom, lifted the window and threw the shoes into the room and onto the sofa. One wonders though, if Mrs Steele knew Mrs Kempson was deaf then did she also know she would often leave her front door on the latch? It may have been usual practice to open a window and 'throw' the shoes in through the window, but it does raise questions.

DCI Horwell noted that in the statements of various people, Mrs Kempson was well known to be deaf, and he also discovered that she frequently failed to answer knocks at the door. It is, therefore, possible that the man seen by Miss Reedes went away, but returned a few minutes later and was then seen by Mr Horn to enter. Moreover, Mrs Kempson had got into the dangerous habit of leaving her front door ajar or on the latch. There was an outside handle to the door, which on being turned would give access to anybody, stranger or otherwise, and owing to Mrs Kempson's deafness it would have been a simple matter to take her by surprise in the back parlour and kill and rob her. Again this is conjecture, though plausible.

But his argument is that Henry was in the house systematically ransacking it and looking for money when Mrs Steele rapped on the door. Mrs Steele unnerved him and he made his escape before he could properly search for money. It might be that this was true, but Henry used a remarkable audacity in some of his schemes, so it is more likely he would observe the front of the house to see Mrs Steele depart. This suggestion is intended to give an alternative view and so demonstrate that there are weaknesses in the police's recreation of the crime.

There is no doubt that the murderer missed some money in the house; one of the drawers containing jewellery in the front bedroom was found locked and undisturbed, the key was in the lock of the drawer below. A small hoard of money was also found in a box on top of the same chest of drawers. The key was in the lock of the box and it was felt that if the murderer had not been disturbed he would have found this small hoard of money. So it was assumed that he got away with only a few pounds. This could be concealing as much information as it was giving, without Mrs Kempson to reveal her hiding places (and she may not have confided in Miss Williams) it is impossible to say just what cash was concealed, found and removed.

In fact, there were some peculiar occurrences in the few months leading up to the murder. The local CID had been involved from October 1930 up to February 1931, probing some rather mysterious events involving petty thefts of some small articles of clothing in the night-time and there was never any evidence discovered to show how the thief entered or left the house. Miss Williams was the victim of some of these thefts and it was believed at the time that Mrs Kempson was responsible, being jealous of Miss Williams spending her time with girls of her own age, thereby neglecting her. Mrs Kempson's mother had recently died and it was known that Mrs Kempson was in a weak state of health and mind. There is little information regarding these incidents, but they are bizarre.

Mrs Steele knew a little about Mrs Kempson's life. She spoke of an insurance agent living in Oxford who about two years before the murder was said to have proposed to Mrs Kempson. It was common knowledge amongst many who knew Mrs Kempson that she was a vain widow who was always remarking that she had male admirers but felt they wanted her money instead of herself.

She had already made a will and the copy was with her brother, Robert. It was also known that she contemplated making another will because her mother, who was included in the first will, had died.

Miss Julia Life described herself as an intimate friend of Mrs Kempson, but it seems strange she also said in her deposition that she had not visited Mrs Kempson for six months. However, she said that she was often able to walk into Mrs Kempson's house without knocking. On Friday evening, 31 July, she met Mrs Kempson in the town and knew that she was going away on the Sunday to London for a holiday on a Varsity bus that passed her (Miss Life's) house. It appears that on Sunday morning, 2 August, Miss Life kept a lookout for the Varsity bus proceeding to London and, failing to see Mrs Kempson among the passengers, she became anxious. So she called at Mrs Kempson's house at 9.30 a.m., 10 a.m., and again at 8 p.m., but failed to get any answer. She tried the front door and found it to be fastened. It seems odd that someone who had not visited her 'intimate' friend for six months should display this level of anxiety for someone who may, quite simply, have changed her travel plans. And was there a reason she had not visited her 'intimate' friend for six months? However, she remained anxious for the remainder of the weekend. At around 9.15 a.m. on Monday 3 August, she called upon Mrs James, wife of Charles James, who had a shop nearly opposite Mrs Kempson's house. Mr James was an occasional gardener employed by Mrs Kempson and held the key of the side gate. Miss Life spoke of her anxiety and requested that Mr James go across to the house to ascertain whether Mrs Kempson was still at home. In the event, he did so and when he came back he said, 'I don't think she has gone as the plants are not out and the breakfast things are on the table in the kitchen.'

He decided to check a second time and went across to Mrs Kempson's house, returned and told Miss Life that he thought it was all right as he had found the plants in the shed. Mr James, who had known Mrs Kempson for many years, ran his small general shop as well as taking on work as a 'jobbing' gardener; he had attended to Mrs Kempson's garden for the past ten years. The mysterious happenings, where small items of clothing and other belongings had gone missing from the house, were something he had heard about through the grapevine rather than from Mrs Kempson. And earlier that year she had shown him some unexplainable footprints in the back garden of her house, which may have been those of woman – but at that time she had not recently missed anything.

Mr James knew that Mrs Kempson usually went to the cemetery on a Saturday afternoon to tidy her husband's grave. This would also be on her agenda prior to her summer holiday every year. By and large, her usual routine after she had been to the grave was to call at Mr James's shop on her return. She had told him of her impending holiday on the Thursday before she was due to go away as she had some ferns in her house she wanted him to mind while she was away. They discussed the arrangements: Mrs Kempson said she would put the ferns outside and Mr James said he would go over probably on the Tuesday or the Wednesday.

On the evening of Saturday 1 August, Mr and Mrs James realised that Mrs Kempson had not called into their shop as was usual on her return from the cemetery. Mr James looked across the road and noticed that both of Mrs Kempson's front gates were open. He also noticed the right-hand sitting room window was open three inches at the bottom. The street door was closed but he did not know whether it was locked or not. Neither Mr nor Mrs James thought there was anything wrong, but Mr James crossed the road and closed the front gates. As he did so, he did not notice anyone loitering about.

As she was going away for two weeks it was possible Mrs Kempson decided to go to the grave at her latest possible opportunity before she left for London. However, this was not the case because on the Bank Holiday Monday morning, 3 August, still remembering that Mrs Kempson had not called into his shop on the Saturday afternoon, Mr James went to the cemetery. It was soon apparent that Mrs Kempson had not attended her husband's grave recently, which seemed to be at odds with her usual routine, even if she was going away. Mr James found Mr Kempson's grave and found the gravestone 'unclean', and there were no fresh flowers on the grave. The flowers he did find were old, and it did not seem as though Mrs Kempson had recently been to the cemetery. He returned home and discussed his observations with his wife. They both felt this was strange; Mr James again looked at Mrs Kempson's house.

This tended to reinforce the view of DCI Horwell that Mrs Kempson had been killed before midday. In fact, if her routine had been as usual, bearing in mind she was about to leave town for two weeks, then it only suggests that if her death had prevented her from attending her husband's grave, then her death occurred before mid- or even late afternoon. And this can be taken a stage further. In his deposition, Mr James said Mrs Kempson was expected to call 'in the afternoon or evening', so it does not suggest Mrs Kempson was dead by midday. Mrs James stated that Mrs Kempson had promised to call into the shop in the afternoon to say 'goodbye' before she went off on her holidays. Again, all of this proves she was not seen by Mr and Mrs James in the afternoon of the 1 August: it does not prove she was dead by lunchtime.

But there is a suggestion that Mrs Kempson had started arranging the ferns for Mr James before she made the beds or cleared the breakfast things as two ferns were found outside the back garden where she said she would put them. There were a dozen or so left in the house so she had only just started, but it does suggest she would leave the bed making and other chores until later. It is also said to suggest that Mrs Kempson was disturbed while this 'job' was carried out.

But the usual routine for Mrs Kempson was to clear away the breakfast things, make the beds and tidy herself up – that is to say take out her hair curlers. But clearly the routine was different this particular day as she had started to take her ferns out of the house before clearing away the breakfast things and making the beds etc. Unless she cleared away the breakfast things and made the beds and decided that as she was going away she could leave her husband's grave (and Miss Williams' bed) until the following day. In short, did something happen to make her change her plans that day?

What we do know is that she opened the door to a man at just before 10.00 a.m. whom she ushered into the house with little ado, not a word passed between them. What a shame Mr Horn, who witnessed this event, was not asked a question that would be in keeping with Mrs Kempson's vanity – 'Was she wearing her hair curlers?'

Part 5

If the folk Mrs Kempson knew in Oxford thought something was not right, then Mrs Annie Smith, the lady Mrs Kempson was to visit, had become alarmed at her failure to arrive. She wrote to Mrs Kempson's brother in Oxford. In those days the postal service had only one class of service but the deliveries were more numerous and covered the seven days.

It was George Reynolds that Mrs Smith wrote to; he had last seen his sister on 22 July, and knew that she intended spending a holiday with a Mrs Smith in West Hampstead, London. He also knew that the lodger, Miss Williams, was going for a week's holiday at about the same time. He knew that his sister was travelling on the Varsity bus on Sunday 2 August.

By the first post on Monday 3 August, he received a letter from Mrs Smith, dated 2 August, informing him that Mrs Kempson had not arrived. On receiving the letter, he went straight to his sister's house but did not get any answer. He sent a telegram back to Mrs Smith in which he said, 'Annie not at home. Wire if any news.'

But later that afternoon, at just about 5.15 p.m., he received a telegram back from Mrs Smith in which she explained that Mrs Kempson had still not arrived. She asked him if he could make some enquiries at the Varsity Coach Company with whom Mrs Kempson had booked her travel. The outcome of these enquiries did not seem encouraging because later that day Mr Reynolds returned to his sister's house, and later still with his son, Albert.

Mr Reynolds himself was now alarmed at his sister's apparent disappearance, so with Albert went to Mr James opposite to obtain the key so they could look around the side and the back of the house. At around 7.20 p.m., they entered the back garden.

They could see that the back, middle bedroom window was open both at the top and the bottom, and the two men thought this would be odd if Mrs Kempson was away. They decided they should investigate further, and Albert managed to find a ladder in his aunt's shed. He climbed up to get into the house through the open window. Albert did not look around the house, but came straight down the stairs to the back door to let his father in. They then started to search the house together.

It is not recorded in what order they conducted their search but when eventually they came to the rear parlour, the door was closed. When they opened the door and entered they found Mrs Kempson inside lying on the floor covered with the doormat and the three cushions. Her face was covered over but there did not seem to be any sign of life. They made to leave the house to seek help and knew they should not touch anything further. Mr Reynolds and his son came out of the house by the front door.

Mr Reynolds said in his statement that the front door was locked and secure. The door could have been fastened in two ways, either by the spring (Yale) lock, or by a lower mortice lock and Mr Roberts was unable initially to give a clear recollection. However, with further questioning it appeared that when he tried to leave the property he put one hand on the key and one hand on the handle of the door, and he thinks he turned both and still could not open the door, but on releasing his hand from the key and turning the Yale lock knob, he was able to open the door. DCI Horwell thought that as Mr Reynolds did not have to turn the key then the street door seems to have been closed just by slamming it and he wondered if that was the action of the murderer when he left the premises.

However, Mr Reynolds eventually left by the front door of the house to summon help. They tracked down the local beat officer, PC Samuel Guyte, and with him they re-entered the house. In his statement, Albert Reynolds corroborated what his father had said in his statement.

PC Guyte confirmed he was approached and, with Mr Reynolds and his son, went to Mrs Kempson's house. He said he entered the house at approximately 7.25 p.m. on the evening of Monday 3 August. He went on to describe what he was shown in the back parlour of the house, that is the body of Mrs Annie Kempson. He carefully removed the cushions and the rug to confirm life was extinct and felt the body was cold and stiff. He noted the wounds. He was careful to replace the cushions and rug in exactly the same position as he had found them. It was also plain to him that there had not been a struggle in the room. However, he did notice that several drawers in the room had been opened. He reported to his station and the police investigation commenced.

One of the first called was the police surgeon, Dr Francis Dickson, who was called in at 8.10 p.m. on the evening of 3 August. Dr Dickson made a report to describe his observations and first examination of the body, which he did at the scene of the crime. He also described his observations when he later assisted Sir Bernard Spilsbury in the post-mortem examination. Dr Dickson stated that he felt the actual cause of death was haemorrhage from the carotid artery, which was severed by a sharp cutting instrument that also penetrated Mrs Kempson's mouth. Therefore, there was a considerable inhalation of blood into the lungs.

However, he stated that death probably took place in the 'forenoon of Saturday, August 1 1931'. But to fast-forward momentarily and consider what Sir Bernard said in his evidence:

From the condition of the body when I saw it on Tuesday, August 4th 1931, she must have been dead for at least twenty-four hours, and her condition then was consistent with her having died on the previous Saturday morning, but not much longer than that. What I found is consistent with the approximate time of death as given by Dr Dixon [*sic*] in his evidence.

There are a couple of points here, without getting bogged down with medical politics, but when Sir Bernard says that she must have been dead for at least twenty-four hours, which means she died on or before Monday 3 August. As she was found on this day, cold and with stiffness (rigor mortis usually sets in after four to five hours, possibly up to seven), then this is stating the obvious. However, in the Oxfordshire Assizes before Mr Justice Swift he said, 'Death might have been on Monday morning … couldn't say it was before Sunday or Monday'. Now, this is not a contradiction because he is saying what was what and not saying one thing was *consistent* with another thing. When doctors say one thing is consistent with another it means it cannot be demonstrated simply that the two things are not related; or it cannot be disproved. Or, more simply, Sir Bernard in his statement said that what Dr Dickson said was consistent (or related) to an approximation (an educated guess) which could not be disproved.

But to get a conviction (that is to say, to convict Henry) the time of death had to be between 9.45 a.m. and 11.00 a.m. (approximately) on the Saturday as this was the time Henry did not have an alibi.

Sir Bernard commented on the death of Mrs Kempson, suggesting that some of the blows were hammer blows and that she was stabbed in the neck whilst lying on her back. At 4.50 p.m. on 4 August, Sir Bernard visited the house and saw the body in the position it was found. Later that day, he conducted a post-mortem examination. His opinion of the cause of death did agree with that of Dr Dickson. Sir Bernard was of the opinion that the deceased was first attacked from behind, a blow being delivered on the back of her head, and the other injuries inflicted while she lay on the ground; she therefore made no attempt to defend herself. He mentions that there would be no spurting of blood and that the spots of blood upon the stockings fell from the weapon as it was withdrawn from the neck. The deceased had no substantial meal on the day of her death. The contents of the stomach suggest that her last meal consisted of food such as bread and butter, and possibly egg or custard. In his opinion, the two larger head wounds, with their associated fractures of the skull, were caused by violent blows with a blunt object having a flat, circular striking surface of about 1¼ inches in diameter, the head of a hammer being the most likely weapon. The wound at the back of the head may have been caused by the same weapon, the thick pad of hair protecting the head from more severe injury. The wound in the neck was caused by a sharp cutting instrument.

In short, the medical evidence did not confirm death had occurred on the morning of the Saturday. It was possible, but not definite.

Portrait of Annie Kempson.

Portrait of Henry Seymour.

Looking towards The Duke public house where Miss Reedes scrubbed the step and observed a man at Mrs Kempson's door.

Oxford Court Buildings. (Copyright Stockphotograph.co.uk)

Part 6

Mrs Kempson was one of five siblings. She was the eldest child of Mr Henry and Mrs Mary Reynolds of Oxford (Mr Reynolds was originally a Wiltshire man), and their only daughter. She was born in 1873, George followed two years later; then Joseph in 1877, Percival in 1879 and Robert was a late chrysanthemum, arriving in 1885. Two of Mrs Kempson's brothers (Robert and George) lived in the Oxford area and the other two (Joseph and Percival) lived in Surrey. It was her brother George and his son who had found her body, but her other brother, Robert, was the one to whom she entrusted the collection of rents from her properties and also attended to her financial affairs. DCI Horwell advised that full enquiries had been made with her bank and her account there was in 'good order'.

Robert Reynolds, who also lived in Headington, said in his statement that all the members of the family were on good terms. It was Robert who Mrs Kempson visited on the Friday evening after she had been shopping with Mrs Steele. He said he last saw his sister at around 8.30 p.m., on the Friday evening, 31 July. She had spoken of her intended visit to London.

On Saturday 1 August, Mr Reynolds had business to attend to and passed his sister's house 'several times' but did not notice anything out of the ordinary. He was out of town himself from 2 August when he travelled to Shanklin on the Isle of Wight where he spent his summer holidays.

In the house on the morning of 1 August, Miss Williams had finished her breakfast and made ready to leave. At 9.30 a.m., she left the house and went to The George Café in the centre of town where she worked. Then, at around 4.20 p.m., she left Oxford. She was aware that Mrs Kempson was due to travel to London the following day.

When Miss Williams left the house she noticed that the front door was unlocked, which meant that anyone could walk in – it would only have been necessary to turn the door handle. This was at around 9.30 a.m. However, it is not clear as to whether the front door was locked or not at just before 10.00 a.m. when Mr Horn saw the man admitted to the house, and when Mrs Steele came to the house with Mrs Kempson's new shoes at around 11.00 a.m. she did not try the front door.

On Miss Williams' return from holiday, the police took her to the house and she made a statement to the effect that everything in the kitchen was as it had been when she left on the Saturday morning – though the ten shilling note she had given as her rent was no longer where Mrs Kempson had put it.

There was half of a loaf of bread on the table and she identified it as similar to what was left after breakfast on Saturday morning, and the police found about 2½ ounces of butter, the remainder of a half-pound packet, lying on the table. Is it possible that this was from the Sunday morning and the loaf of bread was not quite the size Miss Williams remembered? And would the scene in the kitchen be consistent with Mrs

Kempson having had breakfast on the Sunday morning? There was bread and butter found in Mrs Kempson's stomach, which would be consistent with a breakfast-like meal, but there was also a residue which Sir Bernard described as custard – not usually associated with breakfast and not mentioned as constituting what was on offer on that Saturday morning. Could it be possible that the loaf of bread on the kitchen table when Miss Williams saw it prior to her departure on the Saturday morning had an additional couple of slices cut off it on the Sunday morning?

She states that Mrs Kempson was careful with her money and there would have been no need for her to have purchased any more bread as she was going away the following morning, but the money-conscious Mrs Kempson had not cancelled her papers: Monday's newspaper (for the first full day she would have been away in London) was delivered.

The police also found a small paper parcel that contained freshly picked garden peas. Miss Williams stated that Mrs Kempson had picked them in her garden and intended on taking them with her to London. This was a full twenty-four hours or more before she was due to depart, if she wanted the peas enjoyed fresh would it not have made more sense to pick them later, such as on the Sunday morning? This does not prove anything, but it is curious that she picked fresh garden peas at least a day before she went away – Mrs Kempson was not due to travel until the Sunday afternoon so would have had plenty of time to pick them either later on the Saturday or even on the Sunday. But the question also emerges as to whether Miss Williams knew when she picked the peas; there is no mention of them in her statement.

But the most curious fact comes from Miss Williams. She returned from her holiday on 5 August and went to the house, and she describes her bedroom, which she seems to have inspected. But, in her statement and in court, she says it was on the days *after* 5 August that she was actually shown the kitchen, so another day or two for her memory to be exposed to the possibility of resizing the loaf of bread. And as each day was the same at breakfast, could it have been possible she had a good look at the bread on the Friday or the Thursday. Is it usual for a witness in a murder trial to be able to remember a mundane fact for five days? Further, she says it was 'on one of these days' (i.e., the days *after* 5 August) that she was shown the kitchen, so not necessarily 5th August, or the 6th or the 7th... The loaf of bread was actually an exhibit in court to support the argument Mrs Kempson was murdered on the Saturday and so she could not have eaten any more than 'one day's slices', but when she took those slices is anyone's guess because Miss Williams left the house before Mrs Kempson had her breakfast. If she was a lady of habit, as the depositions assert, then it is possible she would put the breadboard in the same place on the breakfast table one morning as she did the next. But it is not certain, nor could it ever be expected to be, to say the breakfast setting in the kitchen was the same as when she left on the Saturday. There has to be the possibility she became convinced the breakfast table was as she left it by either external pressure – such as a policeman asking if it was the same or her convincing herself it was the same. Of course, the expected difference, if the table was laid on a Sunday morning for breakfast, would be that it would be for one, Mrs Kempson. But if her visitor of Saturday, who arrived at about 10.00 a.m., stayed all day and overnight then she may have had two for breakfast on Sunday. This may be making inroads to fantasy, but it is not beyond conjecture: according to the evidence, no person made a statement to say they saw the man leave Mrs Kempson's house that day. Did he even sleep in Miss Williams' bed?

Miss Williams did describe the occurrences in the house where things were removed but with no sign of entry. However, she does not seem to have been able to shed any light on these incidents.

The description of Mrs Kempson's character that Miss Williams gave the police suggested a vain lady and that if a man paid her a compliment then she felt there was a romantic undercurrent. If a man was known to her as a 'charmer' then she might admit him to her house as she was seen to do on the Saturday morning, 1 August. Henry was a salesman who oozed charm and no doubt he knew what ladies would want to hear him say, but this does not prove it was he who entered the house on that Saturday morning.

He worked for the Tellus vacuum cleaner manufacturer but Mrs Kempson had bought her cleaner two years before, and the salesman demonstrated the cleaner in the house. It is known that Henry would 'follow up' and see if the machine was satisfactory but he does not seem to have played a leading part in her conversations with Miss Williams, suffice to being described as a 'nice man.' Miss Williams never actually saw him.

Further, Mrs Kempson was a woman described as unlikely to give money to anyone without a threat of violence. However, this seems superfluous as she seems to have been attacked from behind and overpowered without any clear evidence of confrontation with her assailant. It is unknown if Henry had previously attempted to borrow, cadge, beg, steal, extort or in any other way obtain money from Mrs Kempson.

The friend Mrs Kempson was to visit for her holiday in London was a Mrs Annie Smith whom she had known for nearly thirty years. Mrs Smith lived in West Hampstead but travelled to Notting Hill Gate to meet her. This arrangement had been made over the preceding few months and the details as she understood them would be that Mrs Kempson was expected to travel from Oxford to London on what was known as a 'Varsity' coach. This was due to arrive in London at about lunchtime. Mrs Smith said she waited a long time for her to arrive and then decided she should get in touch with Mrs Kempson's family.

The two had last met the previous May, but wrote to each other regularly.

Mrs Kempson did confide in Mrs Smith. For instance, she described a proposal of marriage she had received. This had been made by a Mr Percy Windle and it was believed he had returned to New Zealand. The police followed this up to confirm.

Mrs Smith could also tell the police that Mrs Kempson usually kept her money in the dining room of her home, either in the sideboard or in a drawer. The most she was thought to have had in the house would be about £5.

Part 7

In his report, DCI Horwell wrote a fairly large piece about the events that led the police to Henry and what factors were relevant to his arrest and charging. He introduces his suspect as 'Henry Daniel Seymour, at one time representative and canvasser for the Tellus vacuum cleaner ...'

Mrs Kempson had bought a Tellus vacuum cleaner from Henry sometime previously. Among what were described as 'the thousand and one articles in this house' Henry's business card was found; it was thought it had been in the position in which it was found for a considerable period. But DS Norman Goodchild followed up this find with some routine police checking. DCI Horwell reported that Henry Daniel Seymour had a criminal record. He said:

> Henry Daniel Seymour, C.R.O. No. 626l/l915, who has a long list of convictions for serious crime ... and who, in June, 1930, attempted to murder Gladys Mary Sloman at 48, Langdon Road, Paignton, Devon, by strangling her and striking her about the head and face with his fist.

Apparently Henry got to know her through the sale of a vacuum cleaner, and after this he went to see her again although the reasons stated did not seem to be in relation to the vacuum cleaner sale.

What happened (according to DCI Horwell's report) was that as Miss Sloman was showing him around part of the house he 'without any hesitation or provocation struck her several violent blows in the face, breaking her teeth, knocking her down and then gripped her by the throat'.

Then she screamed, so he let go of her and fled from the house. There was no claim that the attack was sexually motivated. Henry was arrested the following day and charged with attempted murder – Miss Sloman was said to have been under medical care for a time after the attack though what precisely the 'medical care' consisted of is not clear. At the time of his arrest, Henry made a statement:

> No-one is more sorry for this than I am. Something seemed to have snapped in my brain and something seemed to tell me this woman was my enemy and responsible for my troubles. In a few seconds my brain cleared and I saw I had done something dreadful. I cleared out.

There is no doubting the seriousness of this attack and it was said that the doctor's evidence showed that considerable violence must have been used. Curiously the doctor is quoted to have said 'considerable violence *must* have been used' rather than *was* used. I make this distinction because the evidence is very clear about the attack – assuming it is accurate – but patchy when it comes to the treatment received. And again some explanation is needed for this line of discussion. The police charged him with attempted murder, which should have attracted a lengthy custodial sentence, but when he appeared in court the charge is merely unlawful wounding for which he was bound over, and ordered to pay compensation to Miss Sloman. Now there is a big difference between attempted murder and unlawful wounding, but it demonstrates how a thief and conman, which Henry definitely was, is so easily tarred with the brush of violent (or *very* violent) on poor or possibly exaggerated evidence; and I do not suggest it was Miss Sloman who exaggerated the evidence.

DCI Horwell said, 'One of the conditions ... (was to) pay ... compensation', so one can only wonder what the other conditions were. If the defence had followed an argument that Henry was suffering from a mental illness he could have been detained (indefinitely) under the 1889 Lunacy Act, but there is no mention of this and clearly it was not applied. So the question of how the charge was reduced will stay with us, but one wonders that if the visit was not in relation to the sale of a vacuum cleaner, then what was it in relation to? And who invoked the invitation?

He was ordered to pay Miss Sloman compensation of £10 within twelve months and it may have been pure coincidence that the date of the expiration of the twelve months was the day before the murder of Mrs Kempson. Henry was missing from home and not a penny of the £10 had been paid. The Paignton police were on the point of obtaining a warrant for his arrest for a breach of the conditions imposed upon him. Wherever Henry went he ran up bills – hotels, work by embezzlement, loans and so on – is it really the case he would be that concerned with the compensation order for Miss Sloman and sufficiently concerned to murder to obtain the money?

It is important to stress this was a serious attack on a woman who had shown Henry some trust, but one has to make the distinction between, let's call it an (alleged) unprovoked episode of manual violence, and smashing someone over the head a number of times with a hammer and then forcing a sharp instrument into their neck with such force it cuts about two inches deep. But DCI Horwell said:

> It is thus shown that he attacked a lonely woman in her house and I venture to suggest that had she not screamed he would have murdered her and robbed her. It is difficult to understand what the Court was thinking about to Bind a man over with such a criminal record upon such a serious charge.

He certainly has a point, but one is left wondering if one does not have the full facts.

There is much made of Henry visiting 'lonely' ladies to sell them vacuum cleaners and it is not clear whether this was 'cold calling' or as a follow-up to a customer's response to an advert. But this 'lonely lady' title has to be considered in its context. In those days, women mainly stayed at home and looked after the house and home. Sometimes bachelor brothers and spinster sisters lived together – it was not all husband, wife and family. The men-folk worked considerably longer hours than they would now, and although these days men do know one end of a vacuum cleaner from another, in the 1930s they probably did not. So if one was to sell a household maintenance item then the wife/lady of the house would be the obvious and sensible target. As men had limited knowledge of the bulk of the 'woman's work' at home then they would see a vacuum cleaner perhaps as an unnecessary expense, and one can think of many men who would not have the first idea of the workload – they went out in the morning and by some miracle, two minutes before they came home, the house is cleaned and a meal prepared.

A fifty-four-hour working week was common at the beginning of the twentieth century, and with the Wall Street Crash and the Great Depression at the end of the 1920s, the employment rate was not that great in the 1930s; so it is difficult to formulate any kind of idea at the number of working women, but anecdotally it was said to be few. The Second World War solved the unemployment problem but the point was that salesmen in the 1930s selling household appliances would be better advised to appeal to the women, so DCI Horwell's title of 'lonely women' can be seen to be misleading.

However, to further consider Henry's past. The attack on Miss Sloman took place at her home in Paignton at about 1.30 p.m. on 13 June 1930. Two hours earlier there was another event involving Henry where no violence was used but it was bizarre. A Mrs Harriett Poole had previously bought a Tellus vacuum cleaner and Henry called on her at her home in Paignton and apparently asked if he could 'come inside.' It was usual for the representatives to follow up sales to ensure the machine was working correctly. But when he got in the house the appliance did not seem to be the focus of his attention. He may have been unwell, as he said, 'Do you mind if I sit down? I've got a terrible head.' According to DCI Horwell's report (which would have been based on another officer's record based on Mrs Poole's observations) he sat down and appeared to be agitated. Mrs Poole offered him an aspirin, which he did not respond to. He left shortly after.

But to return to the Oxford episode. The business card was found together with the vacuum cleaner. There were also letters found which related to the Tellus machine and included a receipt for £1 15s 6d, marked 'Paid with thanks', and initialled H. S. DCI Horwell thought this demonstrated Henry had been to Mrs Kempson's house on more than one occasion, and he probably had. And not to forget that whoever was seen entering the house on Saturday 1 August was admitted with little hesitation. But this does not prove that it was Henry.

In 1928, early on in his career with the company, Henry demonstrated a Tellus cleaner to a Miss Wilhelmine Little in Oxford and she decided to purchase the machine. But she did not appear to receive the usual follow-up visits; in fact, she had not seen him again for about two years when he called on her. He was now no longer with the company but was selling ladies' knitted clothing instead. The outcome of this renewed contact between Miss Little and Henry was that she rented him and his wife and son some unfurnished rooms. The rent for this was £1 5s od per week. Unfortunately, paying the rent was not uppermost in Henry's priorities and arrears soon built up. Miss Little went on holiday for over a month and when she returned all was chaos – the rent was even further in arrears and the gas had been cut off (gas being a far more common energy for lighting than today). Not surprisingly, Henry had disappeared. Mrs Seymour gave up the tenancy that August and went to stay with friends in London; Miss Little arranged for their son to stay with some of her friends in Cheshire. The police were finding some quite unpalatable facts about Henry's behaviour, his home life and his business practices.

At this point, they turned their attention to the Tellus company itself. DCI Horwell's team had requested from them all details of the activities of Henry whilst in their employ, including a list of the names and addresses of their customers for the Oxford area. The police waited over three weeks and in the end, following some visits from fairly senior police officers explaining the urgency of the information, they finally acceded. There were over two hundred names and address, and enquiries were made. The outcome of this was the identification of a Mrs Alice Andrews, who was a widow and lived with her son in her bed and breakfast guest house in Gipsy Lane in Headington. This was about three quarters of a mile from Mrs Kempson's house. Mrs Andrews was to become a crucial witness in the case.

Part 8

Mrs Andrews was to play a leading role in Henry's conviction. She had bought a Tellus vacuum cleaner through Henry a couple of years before Mrs Kempson's murder, and since that time he had called at the house from time to time and she had bought other things from him. There is a strange passage in DCI Horwell's report that says:

> ... that in the middle of July, 1931, he called at her house saying that he had had a motor accident six weeks previously and had lost his memory. He told her that he was coming out of a side road and in avoiding a boy he failed to notice a car on tow. He also mentioned that he had been to Bournemouth and Folkestone. He left Mrs Andrews after a few minutes conversation.

Though the accident is mentioned in the depositions and court records, this rather strange visit to Mrs Andrews is not.

Around 2.30 p.m. on Friday 31 July, Mrs Andrews met Henry at the top of Headington Hill as he was coming up; this would mean he was then coming from the direction of Mrs Kempson's house. According to what Mrs Andrews stated, Henry stopped her and was quoted to have said, 'Oh! I should have found you out if I had called'. He went on to say it had been his intention to go bathing in the river at Eynesham but thought the weather might turn 'thundery'. He told her he was then staying in Thame, a small village nearby. They parted and he walked away, it would seem in the direction of Headington.

Later that evening, Henry did call at Mrs Andrews' house, but he was in a predicament. He said he had gone to Eynesham after all but as he left his clothing concealed while he swam, some young boys had robbed him of 30s (£1.50) which was a good sum. He saw them at the last moment and gave chase but they were, he said, too quick for him. As he knew Mrs Andrews and lacked social scruples he asked her quite bluntly if she could lend him some money. Mrs Andrews was quite willing to help him out and when she fetched her bag found she had 5/6d in change:

'Look, this is all the change I have got.'

Henry said, 'I will take four and sixpence.'

So she let him take the money and away he went. As far as Mrs Andrews could see, he had a fawn raincoat with him, but was not carrying anything.

He had said further, 'I am catching the Viking coach to Thame at the booking office up the road at 9.15 p.m.'

Mrs Andrews was a widow and lived with her grown-up son, Percival. He had heard the conversation and when he looked out of his bedroom window he saw Henry hurrying away, he described him as 'half running'.

It was felt by the police that Henry wanted this money to go to an ironmonger where he would buy tools to batter and stab Mrs Kempson to death.

Later that evening at around 10.30 p.m. there was a knock on the door. Mrs Andrews was in bed and Percival would have answered the door that late anyway. Mrs Andrews' house was a guest house, and Henry explained that he had not caught the bus (he did not put his hand out, so it did not stop), so he was stuck. He asked if he could stay the night and Mrs Andrews was quite happy to help. Mrs Andrews made the necessary arrangements and prepared him some cocoa and a light supper. He retired at around 11.15 p.m.

As his mother made arrangements, Percival showed Henry where he could hang his hat and raincoat in the hall. Henry took off his raincoat, but a couple of stories are available as to what happened next.

According to DCI Horwell, quoting from Percival Andrews' statement, as Henry took off his coat:

He was seen to pull from one of the pockets a new hammer and a new chisel, wrapped separately in brown paper which was torn. Henry commented 'I have just bought some new tools' and at the same time he laughed. He put the tools on the floor of the hall. Young Andrews noticed a label on the handle of the hammer and that the chisel was about ¾-inch in width. He saw the blade but not the handle.

However, what Percival later said was significantly different. He said he saw both parcels, and that there was a hammer in one. But he said in his deposition that he did not see what was in the other parcel.

This is an important point because the case against Henry was that he bought a chisel with which he stabbed Mrs Kempson, but Henry said he bought a screwdriver. Yet DCI Horwell said that Percival could actually describe it by width. Without a full trial transcript, it is not possible to know what was said in court, but in the judge's notes there is no mention, nor is there in his summing up, that Percival saw a chisel. That leaves one with the thought that DCI Horwell may have tried to change some evidence.

Mrs Andrews said Henry rose at around 8.00 a.m. the following morning (which was Saturday 1 August) and when he came downstairs he said he would go out to the barber for a shave while she prepared breakfast. He returned about twenty minutes later for his breakfast. As he ate, Mrs Andrews was busy cleaning the hall and noticed the two brown paper packages. She described the contents as a brand-new hammer with a light varnished handle, wrapped in thin brown paper, and a new chisel with light varnished handle, and ¾-inch blade.

DCI Horwell, in stampeding for the scaffold, said, 'It will thus be seen that there can be no mistake. Mrs Andrews and her son saw the hammer and the chisel...'

Well her son did not. If Henry's story was true and he was robbed as he swam, which left him without money, then the question is quite clear, and that is how did he buy the tools (hammer and screwdriver/chisel). There is nothing to prove he did not buy them early in the day and although it was asserted he left Mrs Andrews and ran to the ironmonger's, this was not proved. There was no positive identification of Henry at the ironmonger's and no proof he had bought a chisel. DCI Horwell said that if he bought the tools with the money Mrs Andrews gave him then he would only have had a few pence left for his shave. But this too cannot be, and was not, proved.

With Henry's character and history there is one of two possibilities about what happened as he bathed the previous day – either he was robbed or he was not robbed. Whatever he said could not be relied on, and with all people who lie, it is impossible to know when they are lying or when they are telling the truth.

Mrs Andrews said that at around 9.30 a.m. or 9.45 a.m. that morning, he left her house. He said, 'Thank you very much, I will see you on Monday.'

Henry picked up the hammer and chisel, placed both in the pocket of his jacket or his mackintosh, and left the house. So he now had what he needed to kill Mrs Kempson. It seems strange that he made no attempt to conceal the fact that he had these tools.

DCI Horwell seemed keen to move Henry over the scaffold to the trap door, he wrote, 'It is thus shown, if Seymour's story to Mrs Andrews is true, he must have left her house at 9.30 am, on the morning of 1 August, 1931, possessed of two tools but without a penny in his pocket.'

It is not 'thus shown'. Who knows what he had? He left her house at 9.30 a.m. with the tools in his possession, but as there is no proof of when they were bought, then he may well have had 4/6d minus the cost of the shave, so in the region of 4s. And there is no certainty of what was or was not stolen the previous afternoon. There were two members of staff from the ironmonger's who gave evidence, and neither identified Henry as the man in the shop after around 8.00 p.m. that night. Although the hammer almost certainly came from the shop, there was no record of when or whether a screwdriver or chisel was purchased with it. Henry had the intention of paying for the bed and breakfast Mrs Andrews had furnished. He wrote her a letter on 6 August:

> Dear Mrs Andrews, I have just discovered that I have had this in my pocket since Monday. Life is such a rush with me. Enclosed P.O. Many thanks for your kindness. I hope to call in about 10 days or so when I will pay you for bed, breakfast and supper. Love to Fairy. Yours sincerely,
> Henry Seymour.

He enclosed a postal order for 5/- which was issued at the Brighton (Preston Road) Post Office on 5 August so possibly he got his dates mixed up as the Monday he refers to would be 3 August. But a big issue was made that Henry was lying. DCI Horwell stated:

> Seymour lies in this letter for the postal order was issued at Brighton on Wednesday, 5th August, 1931. Therefore he could not have had it in his possession since Monday. The postmark on the envelope is dated 1.45 p.m. 5th August, 1931.

Fairy, to whom he refers, was Mrs Andrews' little girl.

It is true to say that Gipsy Lane, where Mrs Andrews lived, was within easy walking distance of Fairacres Road, which was where Mrs Seymour was staying with their son. But it is equally important to remember that a warrant had been issued for his arrest for the money he had embezzled from his employer, Yarnstrong's. He may have feared he would be arrested if he went to his wife.

It was also clear Henry had no inclination to 'cover his tracks' for this night and morning with Mrs Andrews. The barber describes him adequately and even remembers the conversation they had, that he had missed his bus the night before and had stayed with Mrs Andrews.

Part 9

It would be of some benefit to just pause to consider the tools Henry had in his possession, both on his person up until the early afternoon of 1 August and also in his luggage at the Greyhound Hotel in Aylesbury. On his person he had a hammer and a screwdriver or chisel. In his luggage, in his hotel room, he had a brace and bit and also a packing case opener. Henry said he had purchased these tools as he thought he could make a living as a woodworker – his profession at the time of his arrest was said to be cabinet maker. There is no evidence that he ever made a living as a woodworker and the fact is a cabinet maker is a skilled trade associated with an apprenticeship. The packing case opener does not fit the profile of a woodworker, so this has to be treated with some scepticism.

However, one 'profession' that would well use a hammer, screwdriver/chisel (probably both) and a brace and bit was something Henry did have experience with: housebreaking. With the old wooden sash-type windows, a hole bored through the frame would give the necessary access for a screwdriver (or other 'thin' tool) to be inserted to open the catch. Henry had a history of opening locks with items other than the keys.

So if one considers 1931, even broadly. The Wall Street Crash had occurred and unemployment and poverty both sides of the Atlantic (and in other directions too) meant that money was in short supply. People could not afford to buy new-fangled electrical appliances (he had left the Tallus Company anyway) and he did not seem to be making a good enough living from selling the garments some of his old customers said they had bought from him. So one answer was to turn to crime, which may more than adequately explain why he was buying the tools – if he were a cabinet maker one would expect him to already own a wide range of tools.

So there is no doubt he had the tools, the doubt is what he intended to use them for. According to DCI Horwell it was to murder Mrs Kempson. So it would be worthwhile to track the hammer (and the screwdriver/chisel) from around midday on 1 August.

At just around 1.00 p.m., Henry returned to the Greyhound Hotel in Aylesbury. In his absence the night before, the landlord, Mr Charles Parkinson, had reported him to the police as missing – Henry had been given a bill earlier which he had not paid. When he arrived at the hotel he said he slipped up to his room and put the hammer and screwdriver/chisel in his luggage. Shortly after this he entered the dining room and asked the maid if she knew where Mr Parkinson was; she soon found him. He advised Henry that he had been reported as missing and the two men should attend the police station. Henry refused and left the hotel to find lunch.

At around 3.30 p.m., PS Leonard Giles visited the Greyhound Hotel and was informed that Henry had returned, but had left again. Mr Parkinson said that as far as he knew Henry's luggage had not been interfered with.

The Sergeant again visited the hotel on Tuesday 4 August, and as Henry was still absent he examined his luggage and noticed a new hammer, a new brace and bit, a new case opener, and other things, but the sergeant did not see fit to take possession of anything. Henry had not retrieved any tools from his luggage, which actually remained at the hotel for another eleven days until PS Reginald Read went to the hotel and took possession of the luggage – a large and a small suitcase. Inside were the tools – hammer, brace and bit and packing case opener – but no screwdriver/chisel. The screwdriver/chisel I will return to.

DCI Horwell examined the hammer and found that it had been 'washed', though it was not considered this was to remove hair, blood, bone or brain. Rather it was that the label had been soaked or scraped off, and that the price details had been almost entirely obliterated by the washing and scraping.

The police went back to the ironmonger's where Henry had not been positively identified as a customer late in the evening of Friday 31 July. However, Mr Alfred Welham, the manager, stated that the tools sold at the shop bore coded pricings, which told the seller the cost and the retail price, and these had been removed. He recognised the hammer as one stocked by the firm and produced an identical item. He said that when the hammer was sold it would have bore a complete 'Heart Brand' label, as well as the pricings – faint traces of these were still present. The hammer had been priced at 1/6d.

The usual time for closing the shop on Fridays was 8.00 p.m., but Friday 31 July was close to a Bank Holiday, and probably the shop was open for a little while after 8.00 p.m. Mr Welham distinctly remembers that a few minutes after 8.00 p.m. on that Friday evening, a man was in the shop being served with a hammer. He was attended to by Mr A. E. Fulkes who had not had much experience in the business: he was the brother of the owner of the shop who was away on holiday.

The man also asked for a bevelled edge chisel and this witness assisted Mr Fulkes by finding a parcel of 1-inch bevelled chisels, which he placed on the counter. That parcel had contained three. He remembers selling one on 30 July, to a regular customer and at the time of making the statement that only one was left in the parcel. As the transaction probably took place after proper closing time, the cash register had been cleared and the paper recording roll had been removed. He was, therefore, unable to find a record of the sale of the hammer and chisel. He remembers replacing the box from which the hammer had been taken, after the shop had been closed for the night. No mention is made of any inquiry as to the sale of a screwdriver.

Henry never denied that he bought tools on 31 July, but he was adamant he had purchased a screwdriver and not a chisel; and if he said he had placed them in his suitcase at the Greyhound Hotel in Aylesbury then that is where they were found, or should have been found. But one wonders about the screwdriver/chisel. It would not be the first time a piece of evidence has 'changed', and as one cannot turn a screwdriver into a chisel, then it might be easier if it were lost.

DCI Horwell examined the contents of Henry's suitcases and in one he found a few small fragments of paper, which appeared to have been scraped off an object. He moistened them, spread them out, and pasted them onto a sheet of white paper. What was produced was an identical pattern to the one shown in Mr Fulkes' store.

It might seem odd and possibly obsessive to remove labels from tools in this manner, but would someone intending to use the tools for housebreaking act in such a way? For the reason that if they were disturbed and needed to 'scarper', then, if they left the tools behind, tracing would be less easy. It is true this would apply to murder also, but it can be proved Henry had a history of housebreaking, and this entire piece is to throw doubt on whether or not he had a history of murder!

The shop was about seven or eight minutes' walk from Gipsy Lane where Mrs Andrews' house was, which brings us back to what Mrs Andrews and her son saw in the brown paper parcels.

Henry mentions that when he went to Mrs Andrews' he took with him a screwdriver and a hammer, which he had purchased on that Friday at an ironmonger's on the corner of a street at Headington. He placed the tools in the hall. He said that he bought the tools because he was a skilled woodworker and he had an idea of obtaining a living by the aid of the tools, but there is a lot of room to doubt what he said.

But it does leave two dilemmas. Firstly, and briefly as it is a matter to return to, the hammer DCI Horwell obtained from PS Giles who had taken it from Henry's luggage was probably not the hammer/weapon which caused the injury to Mrs Kempson's head. Secondly, there seems the problem or riddle of the missing screwdriver/chisel. But since we are back with Mrs Andrews and Percival, her son, it is a relief that Percival was said to have seen the chisel in the brown paper parcel in the hall of his mother's house that night. And so clear was his memory of it that, according to DCI Horwell, 'Nothing will shake Mrs Andrews and her son in their evidence. When son was seen he was able to draw a sketch of the bevelled blade of the chisel. It was so clear in his memory.' The deposition made by Percival Andrews is worth considering then. These are the relevant parts:

As he (Henry) was hanging them up (hat and coat) he took out of a pocket of the raincoat two packages, one of which contained a hammer of which I saw part of the head and the whole of the handle. The head was of bright metal. The part I saw was wedge shaped and the opposite end to the striking end, and the handle was new wood, varnished with a label stuck diagonally across it. The other parcel was well wrapped up and I did not see what was in it.

He did not see what was in it.

In sum, in trying to track the tools Henry may or may not have bought at Mr Fulkes' ironmonger's shop on 31 July, one finds a hammer (with peeled label in his luggage) and a screwdriver/chisel, which a witness does not see, yet sketches. One wonders what became of the sketch.

Part 10

There are a few other issues about Henry's behaviour that need some discussion, for one thing there is the reason why he had a hotel room in Aylesbury yet spent a night with Mrs Andrews in her bed and breakfast accommodation; although Mrs Andrews' house was described as a mere 'comfortable walk' from the home Henry had set up at Mrs Little's with his wife and son.

It is unclear whether Henry had left his wife pending a permanent parting or whether he was 'on the run' from a possible warrant for his arrest regarding the embezzlement of funds from Yarnstrong's. It is more likely to be the latter, and a warrant was to be issued for his arrest.

But on the day he moved from the flat he shared with his wife, he was involved in a motor accident. He had hired a car. The accident happened at around 9.15 a.m. on 26 June, and the matter was reported to DCI Horwell by the Oxfordshire Constabulary. The accident happened at a crossroads in the village of Stanton St John, which is to the north-east of Oxford. Henry was driving his hired Morris Oxford and was in a collision with a vehicle that was being towed by another. The car sustained minor damage to its front bumper and radiator, but there were no personal injuries to the occupants of either car. True to form though, the details Henry gave the police were false – he said he was a Mr Seyton of Gipsy Lane in Headington. When the police looked into things, Henry had actually given the hire company the details of his wife's address at Fairacres Road in Oxford.

The police went to the address in Fairacres Road and found Mrs Seymour, but she told them that Henry had disappeared on the day of the accident. With the address and the details he had given the hire company, and the various references Henry made to people regarding the accident, the police had little doubt it was him.

Little further happened until 14 August, when the connection was made between the accident and Henry's travels around Oxford and the Aylesbury end of Buckinghamshire, and importantly for the police, the luggage left by the missing resident from the Greyhound Hotel in Aylesbury.

Mr Parkinson, the landlord of the Greyhound Hotel, had reported his resident missing and a PS Giles had taken the details. The resident had booked in as a Mr R. Seymour of Exeter. PS Giles had looked in the luggage Henry had left behind at the hotel and noticed the tools: the packing case opener, the hammer and the brace and bit (the screwdriver/chisel seems to have gone missing). This information was put with details given by Mrs Andrews and the staff at Fulkes' Ironmonger's. A description was taken which, the police said, corresponded with the man seen entering Mrs Kempson's house on the morning she was said to have been murdered. There was a warrant out for Henry's arrest on the embezzlement charge. The problem now facing the police was how to trace him.

But when the police searched Henry's belongings, a piece of blotting paper was found which was indented with an address in Brighton. The Brighton police were contacted and when Henry arrived at the flat he had rented they were waiting to arrest him. He was arrested on the warrant issued on 11 August regarding the alleged embezzlement of funds from Yarnstrong's.

However, he was again arrested on 15 August at just after 1.00 p.m. by DS Percy Scales and two other officers who had approached him and said, 'We are police officers, you are wanted by the Metropolitan Police, your name is Seymour.'

Henry shook his head and said, 'You have made a mistake.'

DS Scales was able to tell Henry a lot more than he thought:

'You are Seymour and you use the name of Harvey.'

DS Scales actually took off Henry's hat to reveal his lack of hair and said, 'I am satisfied.' Henry had suffered an illness in his teenage years which resulted in hair loss that would never grew back.

On his arrest he was taken to Brighton Police Station. He was not told why he was wanted by the police and does not appear to have been cautioned. This caused some consternation later.

DCI Horwell heard of the arrest and made arrangements to travel to Brighton. He arrived there on Sunday 16 August and, at around 3.30 p.m., accompanied by DS Rees, he saw Henry in the cells. Henry was formally cautioned; he said, 'Go on, play your cards on the table and tell me what you want me for and tell me your name.'

DCI Horwell introduced himself: 'I am Chief Inspector Horwell and this officer is DS Rees.'

Henry replied, 'Yes, now carry on, Mr Horwell. Is it about this murder at Oxford?'

'Yes, I have been investigating the case. Your visiting card was found on Mrs Kempson's mantel piece and an electric sweeper, sold to her by you, was found in the house. A man answering your description, carrying a light raincoat, was seen at her door shortly before 10 a.m. on the Saturday before August Bank Holiday, the day she was last seen alive, and I am informed that on the previous night you stayed with Mrs Andrews at Gipsy Lane, not far from Mrs Kempson's house. You told Mrs Andrews that you had no money and borrowed four and sixpence from her, and I find that you went out and returned with a new hammer and a new chisel. The hammer has been traced to your possession. Some money is missing from Mrs Kempson's house and I find that you reached Brighton with money on the day of her death, and in consequence you will be taken back to Oxford and charged with the crime.'

Henry responded by saying, 'Right, now I know the state of affairs, I suppose it is my turn to explain my side of the situation.'

DCI Horwell went on to say, 'You quite understand the caution, and if you like Sergeant Rees will write down what you have to say.'

Henry replied, 'My head has been dizzy these last few weeks and what with my motor accident and my bad nerves I shall have to think very slowly and that will give you time to write every word I want.'

Henry went on to make a statement which was taken down for him, at the end of which it was read over to him and he signed it. DCI Horwell had remained present while he made his statement. The statement itself is long and rambling but the points he made can be recorded here more succinctly.

Henry freely admitted he knew Mrs Kempson and had met her through the selling of a vacuum cleaner about eighteen months previously. He mentioned his car accident but became a bit vague regarding dates, but the accident is described in the context of him leaving Oxford so it is at the time he 'left' his wife and son. He described how he took the lodgings in Brighton and that he left there to go to Aylesbury on 22 July. His landlady was Mrs Belmore and he had quickly (and as usual) become in arrears with his rent. Henry was adamant that he went from Brighton to the Aylesbury/Oxford area to collect money and cited a few instances when he had done so, giving the names and addresses of the customers. Whilst in the area he described his base as the Greyhound Hotel in Aylesbury. He also attempted to collect money in the Oxford area and stated he saw a maid at the residence of a Mrs Thomas, but there is no mention as to whether he actually collected money here or not. Again he was vague regarding dates.

One issue he discussed in some detail was the alleged bathe he took at Eynesham during which he was robbed. After this he went to Headington where he called on Mrs Andrews. He said he told her what had happened at Pynk Hill, and then borrowed four and sixpence from her.

Henry said that when he left Mrs Andrews he went and spoke to the agent for the Viking Bus Company at Headington, where he made enquiries about the bus to Aylesbury. His vagueness about dates may have been genuine because he describes this evening as the Friday when he lost his money, though he knew that it was between 8.00 and 9.00 p.m. But he discovered that the bus only went as far as Thame, which was way short. He therefore decided to return to Mrs Andrews, where he arranged to stay the night.

He also told the officers in his statement that when he went to Mrs Andrews he had with him a hammer and a screwdriver, which he had purchased on that Friday from an ironmonger's; the shop being on the corner of a street in Headington. This almost certainly refers to Fulkes'. And Henry said he left the tools in Mrs Andrews' hall. The following morning he rose, had his breakfast and had a long chat with Mrs Andrews, explaining that when he left he would be heading straight back to Aylesbury. It was a Bank Holiday weekend.

But he did not go straight back to Aylesbury. Instead he went to Bexley House, which is in Old Headington where Revd Ernest Green lived with his wife. But then he remembered that he had been told not to visit in the morning. He therefore changed his plans again and went to the Viking Bus Office, which was in Headington, but found there would be a fairly long wait for a bus to Aylesbury. He therefore decided to walk to Wheatley, which is about four miles.

When he got to Wheatley, Henry went to an inn where he talked to the landlord, after which he was able to get a bus and travelled on to Aylesbury, and then to the Greyhound Inn. On his arrival, he went up to his room and used the toilet, then washed his hands. He put the hammer and screwdriver into his luggage as he did not want to carry them about with him. He went downstairs and asked the maid if she would be good enough to find Mr Parkinson, the landlord, for him.

Both Mr and Mrs Parkinson told him that he had been reported to the police as a missing person. He said this made him nervous; he got the 'wind-up' over the trouble he had found himself in with Yarnstrong's. As there had been some police involvement, or at any rate talk of the police, he left the hotel and went to a local restaurant to have lunch. After this he caught the 'Premier' bus for London. He said the time by now was getting on for 2.00 p.m.

As for the tools he bought, he said that he bought them because he was a skilled woodworker and he had an idea of obtaining a living by the aid of the tools. How close to the truth this is, or for that matter how distant, is something that can only be guessed at. Henry travelled on to London where he caught another bus to take him down to Brighton. He paid his landlady, Mrs Belmore in Brighton, £1 for the rent.

Henry was adamant that during the whole of his time in Oxford, particularly when he was in the Headington area, he did not knock or call on Mrs Kempson, nor did he see her out from her house.

About two days before he was arrested, Henry paid Mrs Belmore another £1 2s 0d towards his rent. He was to receive some money through the post, £1, which was sent by a Miss Timms in Oxford.

At the time of his arrest, the police took possession of his clothing, which yielded few clues as to his involvement or otherwise in the murder of Mrs Kempson, though there was a 'stain' in the coat pocket that was brought to his attention – he said he had put some meat he had bought from a butcher into his pocket.

Henry had read about the murder of Mrs Kempson as it was well covered in the newspapers, but he denied most emphatically having any involvement in it, and he told the police that all he knew about it he had read in the newspapers. The journalists had been quick to cover the story and they also sought information from people who were to become witnesses, this was a point the prosecution were to rely on.

Part 11

Henry Seymour's semi-chaotic, semi-secret, semi-concealed, semi-fictitious, but largely dishonest lifestyle had taken him to Brighton.

It has often been said that salesmen sell themselves first and then introduce the product once they have their 'prey' well groomed. If this is true – which is speculative and anecdotal – then one wonders about the 'friendships' they develop as this process unfolds. In Henry's case, he seems to have been endeared to several ladies in the story, but there is little or no information about ladies he attempted to demonstrate or sell the Tellus vacuum cleaners or clothing to, but from who he received a polite (or impolite) 'no thank you'. And again speculating with having no information to qualify the idea, some salesmen might have used the knowledge they acquired from potential or actual customers, about the locks and layout of their homes; and whether they were married, with children, or other residents. This unscrupulous information collection might also include finding a useful place on a window to drill through the wooden frame with a brace and bit before the screwdriver twisted in to open the window. Burglar alarms were not a problem for burglars in those days! Moreover, in Henry's case it seems one lady lent him money with very little persuasion, were there others who gave him similar or other favours?

So if there is any truth of selling yourself first and then letting the product follow, can this be supported by other marketing techniques? A new car, for instance, sporty or otherwise, usually comes with some suggestion that the 'image' of the purchaser will be enhanced; in short, if you buy this car then you are likely to find a twenty-year-old blonde sitting on the bonnet. If you buy this aftershave then be prepared to be chased by several hundred skimpily-clad women. What is pleasing to the eye will sell, or help to sell.

Pausing briefly, it was said that Mrs Kempson admitted the visitor to her house on 1 August with no conversation passing between them. So they knew each other, and she welcomed him with little ado. Taking the clock back a little and thinking about the *modus operandi*, if it was Henry who knocked on the door at about ten minutes to ten and then went away, it would not establish the probability of no one in the house – Mrs Kempson was deaf and might not have heard. So the intruder could well be assessing if Miss Williams was at home. The point is that if Mrs Kempson took her visitor in so willingly, then with Henry's level of charm, would he not, as many of her friends did, just open the door and walk in? But whoever did knock on the door at ten minutes to ten that morning established that Miss Williams was not in.

By mid-August, or at any rate when the police caught up with him, Henry was in Brighton with a new flat, a new landlady and a new name. The police interviewed Mrs Isabel Belmore of Preston Park, Brighton. She let the three upper rooms in her house as a furnished flat, and on 8 July she agreed to rent the flat to Henry – the rent was £1 2s od per week; he took up residence on 9 July 1931.

He said his name was Mr Harvey and described himself as a journalist. He wanted a longer rather than a short-term rental as his wife was to join him later. Mrs Belmore told the police that he did not seem to do much, and stayed in bed until late morning. His rent fell into arrears as a matter of course. However, on 22 July, he left the flat quite early in the morning and said that he was going to London and would return in a day or two. She did not hear from him for over a week. Late in the afternoon of 1 August, Mrs Belmore received a telegram: 'Returning 8.30 tonight. Harvey'. As a matter of fact he returned at 8.00 p.m. He had a raincoat with him. Mrs Belmore said he seemed agitated and when she asked him if he needed any necessities for the Bank Holiday weekend he seemed to have difficulty in concentrating on things. She went on to say that he put his hands to his forehead and said, 'I cannot think, I am so worried. My wife has gone off to America.'

But he paid Mrs Belmore a £1 note for the overdue rent, and soon after went out to purchase his groceries, Mrs Belmore lent him a paper carrier for that purpose. When he returned to the flat he told Mrs Belmore that whilst on the train journey down from London another passenger stole his luggage. This was completely untrue.

As was often the case, wherever Henry went, something bizarre was not too far away. On 12 August, Mrs Belmore was to discover two holes in the ceiling of her bedroom, which was directly underneath the sitting room of Henry's flat. On 14 August, she asked him if he knew anything about these holes but he could only mumble something about it looking as though someone had been trying to 'saw through'. Mrs Belmore's patience seems to have run short, as she told him he was a 'shifty man' and that he had better leave. She made her displeasure at the rent arrears known and so Henry paid her a week's rent there and then. The police were later able to take possession of the money he paid her with. And on the following day, Saturday 15 August, he borrowed half a crown (2s 6d 12½p) from her!

On the Sunday morning after he returned (2 August) she remembered a larger-than-usual amount of water and soap suds came through the pipes from his rooms. Following his arrest, Mrs Belmore went into the front room of the flat he had rented and examined the floorboards. She found there were two holes in the floorboards that seemed to correspond in their position with the two holes in the ceiling of her bedroom, below. They had not been there when Henry moved in and it was difficult to imagine anyone else wishing to drill or make the holes.

There was another resident in the house, a lady of Austrian nationality – Miss Hedwig Ranth – who also recorded her observations about her fellow tenant. Apparently

Henry had said to her, 'You know, sometimes we are all mad', but there is no further information to judge the context in which this was said. However, he did tell her about his motor accident, and described how his luggage had been stolen from the train. Miss Hedwig is quoted to have said that she thought Henry was not in his 'right senses'.

Mrs Belmore produced a letter for the police that had been written by Henry sometime earlier, it was dated 26 July and bore an Aylesbury postmark. It was signed as 'F. Harvey'. He said he was seeing the doctor for his heart and he was to be examined every day. So he sent her a postal order for 12s 6d in respect of his rent. He mentioned the road accident of the previous month and concluded with saying, 'Everything depends upon the result of the medical examination. I am very much upset.'

Part 12

I mentioned that Henry's landlady stated that there was an unusually large amount of water and soap suds coming from his rooms to the drains. This may or may not be significant. There may have been some blood on the murderer's clothing, although this would have been a small amount. The police also made an issue of the labels being washed off the tools Henry had bought. These two issues do not take us very far. Firstly, if Henry was the killer then one would look for previous records. Of course, he attacked Miss Sloman but on that occasion he used his fists and 'gripped her by the throat'. He did not use a weapon. But it also demonstrates that he may have favoured some form of strangulation rather than a hammer to the head and stabbing with a screwdriver/chisel. Secondly, if he knew Mrs Kempson would invite him into her house and lead him through to where she entertained her guests, even a neck tie neatly rolled in his pocket could have proved just as effective in the murder. He made no attempt whatever to conceal the tools, and going back to Mrs Belmore and the possibility that he was washing the label or possibly blood from the hammer and screwdriver/chisel, it was well documented that he placed them in his luggage at Aylesbury and left the hotel without them before he travelled to Brighton. The luggage was untouched for about a fortnight until the Buckinghamshire police investigated at the Greyhound Hotel and found a hammer together with shreds of paper, which later proved to be the label. And as the police now had Henry's hammer this brings up two points – the first being that it travelled from Oxford to Aylesbury and no further. However, also and far more to the point, when Sir Bernard Spilsbury examined the wound on Mrs Kempson's head, and then measured the striking surface of the hammer, he came to the conclusion that this hammer had not been used to inflict the blows on her head.

Returning just a moment to the rather excessive use of water and soap suds from his room, he may have been cleaning blood from his coat. But examination of his coat along these lines did not reveal anything conclusive.

Forensic science/medicine does not forget its evidence, nor does it alter it and it does not lie. On the other hand, evidence reasonably collected by the police can rely on the human element, so mistake and memory come into the arena, not to mention any manipulation or misrepresentation. DCI Horwell's report was detailed and showed the thoroughness of the investigation. But one area where they did not stand any chance of obtaining even a blurred picture of events was when they tried to investigate Henry's activities by making an 'endeavour to sum up his expenditure on that day and the few succeeding days up to the date of his arrest'.

This is because Henry would make a mistake, suddenly develop a poor memory, lie, misrepresent and manipulate. So if he said he had two shillings in his pocket he could just as possibly have had two pence or two pounds. DCI Horwell, when he takes up this part of the story, takes as his starting point when Henry borrowed 4s 6d from Mrs Andrews on 31 July. He said he had been robbed whilst bathing at Eynesham – whatever Henry said about the money he had in his possession would almost certainly be inaccurate.

Mrs Kempson was going on a fortnight's holiday the day after she was murdered, and with not even a hint of an ATM at her bank, she would have had to be in possession of any cash for said holiday on the Saturday morning. It would be reasonable to assume Mrs Kempson may therefore have had anything from £2 10s to £3 in her possession. Plus there was the ten shilling note Miss Williams had given her as rent. But as for what Henry had had in his possession, or what had been stolen or otherwise from him, it's anyone's guess. So any demonstration of income and outgoings is highly unlikely to be accurate.

It is worth, just for a moment, considering Henry's overall financial situation. He was said to be in debt for 'a considerable amount for a man in his station in life'. But this assumes he had not secreted some money away somewhere and there is little mention of any kind of extravagant lifestyle, or paternity payments, gambling problems or any other elements that may have led to the description of 'financially embarrassed'. There is mention of his debt but no details as to accurate figures (figures verified by his creditors). Statements were taken from a variety of people to whom he owed money but his debt would have far exceeded what he was likely to net from a widow's house in Oxford. As for the lady he assaulted in Devon, Miss Sloman, he had been bound over to pay her £10 in compensation but had not done so – he was supposed to have paid this within twelve months of the court order, but he only had a day or two left. And as well as this there was the criminal liability to his employers, possibly Tellus Ltd, but certainly Yarnstrong Ltd.

On the morning of 1 August, Henry was said to be at the 'end of his tether' with a big issue made of having no money in his pocket, but a hammer and chisel. But there is not, nor can there ever be, any vaguely accurate approximation as to the money he had in his possession. Henry was a skilled housebreaker with the tools to do his job, and the CV to demonstrate he did not do it well sometimes – overall he had attracted aggregated prison sentences of nearly twenty years. Getting convicted for housebreaking or shop burglary is more of an 'occupational hazard' than the law-abiding community tend to think.

Although he was said to have left Mrs Andrews' house at about the same time that Miss Williams was leaving the house of Mrs Kempson. It seems likely these two facts are coincidental.

I do not seem to be the only individual to have suspected Miss Williams, Mrs Kempson's lodger. Can it be verified that what Miss Williams said about her last moments with Mrs Kempson was true? Not exactly, but it was made clear in DCI Horwell's report that the police did bear in mind that Miss Williams may have been the last person to see Mrs Kempson alive in the house, and what he described as 'exhaustive enquiries were made surrounding her movements on the morning of 1 August 1931'.

As a consequence of this, DCI Horwell and his colleagues were satisfied that she had nothing to do with the crime. He went on to list some of her characteristics: that she was of slight build and 'weak' but with a pleasant disposition. However, it did not stop there as he described statements taken from her colleagues at The George Café in Oxford – three waitresses and the head waiter were interviewed and this, DCI Horwell submitted, would 'rule' out Miss Williams as a suspect.

Part 13

This would be as good a place as any to look at what Henry said he was doing between around 9.45 a.m. to 11.00 a.m. on the morning of 1 August 1931.

It is fairly well established that he left Mrs Andrews' house at between around 9.30 and 9.45 a.m. In her deposition, Mrs Andrews actually said the time he left was 9.30 a.m. He was next 'positively identified' by another old customer, Mrs Florence Collins, at a bus stop at, she said, between 11.00 and 11.30 a.m. These are both positive identifications as they are by people he knew; and knew him, and there is also recorded conversation so there is not much room for doubt that it was Henry.

And without breaking down the travelling time, on foot, from Mrs Andrews' house to Mrs Kempson's and then to the bus stop where he was seen by Mrs Collins, it would have given him well over an hour to commit the crime. This assumes that the estimated time of death was between 10.00 and 11.00 a.m. on Saturday 1 August. This does not completely accord with the pathologist, but is within the time range. Dr Dickson, who first examined Mrs Kempson at the scene of the crime, asserted that Mrs Kempson's usual routine for breakfast was certainly evident from what he saw at the house on that Saturday morning. Without losing track and thinking the worse, it is doubtful he would know what the morning routine was in Mrs Kempson's house unless he was a frequent visitor in the morning. He might have assumed that what he saw in the kitchen was the usual set up for a breakfast, and he may well have been right, but that does not prove he saw the Saturday scene. Miss Williams said, when she returned to the house on (or she says after) 5 August, that the breakfast things were exactly as she had left them – an almost incredible feat of memory. Possibly she may have thought that what she saw in the kitchen showed the usual routine for breakfast in the house. It is possible the scene as recorded by Dr Dickson and Miss Williams does point to a Saturday morning slaying, but it is also possible that it does not.

So the bus stop at which Mrs Collins saw Henry is about a twenty-minute walk from Mrs Kempson's house. According to DCI Horwell, Henry was in an 'agitated state' and his behaviour was 'peculiar': 'he was in such a state that he wanted to get on any bus, even Mrs Collins' bus, which was not going his way.'

In his summing up, the judge skimmed over this bit, as it was conjecture on the part of DCI Horwell. Henry may have been agitated and seemed peculiar but this does not prove it was because he had just battered Mrs Kempson to death. And one wonders if 'agitated' and 'peculiar' were actually used in Mrs Collins' deposition; but did Mrs Collins confirm Henry was 'in such a state that he wanted to get on any bus, even Mrs Collins' bus, which was not going his way'?

This is an exaggeration of the facts as can be shown. The following is from Mrs Collins' deposition, it is not complete, but representative and the quotes are exact:

> I saw the accused. I said 'Good morning' to him and he replied 'Good morning'. He said 'I am going on my holidays to Brighton.' I then saw my 'bus coming and he said he would get on it and I told him it was leaving the main road ... I cannot say if there was any mark on the front of the 'bus showing that it was going to the Wingfield. I know the bus ... because of the time. When I told him ... he said 'I will walk to Green Road'. I know that the 'Varsity' buses go from Headington to London which are not the same colour as the Wingfield buses. He was very nervous and agitated which was very different from other occasions on which I had seen him.

DCI Horwell's claim that Henry was in such a state that he wanted to get on any bus, even Mrs Collins' bus, which was not going his way ...' is not true if taken from what Mrs Collins actually said, Henry may have thought the bus went somewhere Mrs Collins knew it did not. He did seem nervous and agitated according to what she says, but the last sentence 'He was very nervous ... which was very different ...' is worth a quick consideration. After the atmosphere of informality as she judges Henry, suddenly comes the phrase 'very nervous' and 'very different'. The question arises here of how this information was gleaned from the witness; there are several ways of asking the same question: 'how would you describe his level of relaxation?' or 'would you describe him as ...?' or 'would you describe him as very ...?' Whatever the case, DCI Horwell misrepresents Henry and the entire scene and then misquotes the witness.

This is important because it is the first contact Henry had after the killing he was accused of. Mrs Collins and Henry were talking, she said, for about five minutes, and she bases her judgement of his nervousness and agitation on this conversation, but she does not quote one thing he said that supports this judgement.

But in the event he did not immediately find the Varsity bus that would take him to Aylesbury on its way to London. Rather he decided to visit another customer in Headington. He said he went to Revd Ernest Green's house in Old Road, but on his arrival he suddenly remembered he was asked not to call there in the mornings. But DCI Horwell considered the reason for his journey there, he had sold Revd Green a Tellus vacuum cleaner but 'that must have been a long while ago', and Henry had left the Tellus company. Revd Green told the police that he knew Henry but could not recall telling him not to call in the morning. His wife said the same. Mrs Ivy Busby, their cook, said she had bought items of clothing from Henry and the last visit he made to the house was between 11.00 and 11.30 a.m. on 30 June 1931. So when DCI Horwell suggests or hints that Henry had no recent business at Revd Green's home, he is again not accurate, and Ivy Busby is quoted to have said that he must not call at the house again, which is not supported by what she said in her deposition. So Henry's activities that morning are unfortunate as an alibi is not established.

Henry walked to Wheatley, which would have taken him about an hour and five minutes, but the police were adamant he had caught the bus. This would mean they could reconcile his activities that morning with the timings given by Mrs Andrews, Mrs Collins *et al.* and allow for a trip to Revd Green's. But if the police were so insistent he caught the bus, then it seems strange that a deposition from any bus driver or passenger is not recorded.

The bus from Oxford was due at Wheatley at around 12.20 p.m. and just a few minutes after that time a man (answering to Henry's description) entered the Kings Arms. The man had two gins and ginger beer, which the judge said was to calm his nerves after the murder. If this were true then the landlord, Mr Geoffrey Hall, would be able to corroborate this. Mr Hall said a man came into his bar just after the bus had arrived, and his behaviour was 'peculiar' but when in court he could not see that man – *Henry was in the dock.* DCI Horwell said the man on the bus (not seen by the driver) and the man in the pub (not recognised by the landlord) was 'undoubtedly Seymour'.

But did he get a good enough look at the man in his bar drinking gin and ginger beer? Mr Hall could describe his clothing and there was the mackintosh over his left shoulder. He remembered what the man drank, and the price, and that he asked about the next bus to Aylesbury. He described the man's behaviour as 'peculiar' and 'restless': 'he walked across the bar and looked through the passage on to the road'.

He also remembered the man opened a conversation about the mines in South Africa, mentioned Johannesburg and Pretoria, and remarked that he had been sent there by the *Australian Argus* to write about the mines. The landlord had to hurry him off to catch his bus for Aylesbury. It probably was Henry as such a lot seems to fit, but Mr Hall said in court that 'I do not recognise anyone in the court as that man'.

What happened to Henry that morning is not clear, but what time Mrs Kempson was murdered is not clear either. The evidence against Henry does not seem as convincing, but there is always more than one way to describe any event. The whole police case and prosecution argument, supposedly backed up by the witnesses who saw the man enter Mrs Kempson's house or were in its environs just before 10.00 a.m. on 1 August; together with Dr Dickson's and Miss Williams' assessment of the breakfast scene being of Saturday and no other morning, leave room for doubt that the whole story is as it was presented.

So if Mrs Kempson was murdered between 10.00 a.m. and 11.00 a.m. on Saturday 1 August then no one would have seen her alive after this time – if one person said they saw her, then this could throw the entire police and prosecution case out of the window. So now I can consider the eleven people who claim to have seen Mrs Kempson, and some even spoke to her *after* 11.15 a.m. on Saturday 1 August 1931.

Part 14

Inevitably, when a serious crime is committed the police will look at the local villains and ask questions in their world. Sometimes this gets results or may lead to a result. In this case it largely ruled out any and all local thieves and suspects because extensive activity and investigation saw the majority give satisfactory accounts of their activities that morning.

DCI Horwell records that many potential witnesses had made statements to say they had seen Mrs Kempson after midday on 1 August, although the police assertion was that this was after the time of her death. If this is so then Henry, who was at the Greyhound Hotel at just after 1.00 p.m. that day, must therefore have an alibi. The idea is that the witnesses who said they saw Mrs Kempson after 1.00 p.m. went against the picture the police wished to paint. Or, put more simply, they did not want to consider anyone else except Henry so any potential evidence which weakened their case had to be scrutinised. It is to be expected though for the police to scrutinise evidence, but 'scrutinise' is a different word to 'devalue'. And when DCI Horwell listed the witnesses involved, he left some of them off the list.

So it is necessary to consider what these witnesses said they saw and then see if other evidence supports it or negates it. One main issue for DCI Horwell was the timing of death. He bases this on the evidence of Dr Dickson who said Mrs Kempson's breakfast things were not cleared, which Miss Williams appears to corroborate. It may be that Dr Dickson did have a good knowledge of Mrs Kempson's breakfast arrangements and he could differentiate between what she would have laid out for her breakfast on the Saturday morning and how that differed to what she would lay out on a Sunday. But as Miss Williams pointed out, the scene was just as she left it five or six days previously; but for a moment or two one might consider what was thought to be supportive evidence to this. On the Friday night, Miss Williams had come home after 10.00 p.m. and heated some milk; she maintained the saucepan was left unwashed. Also there was the fact that two cups had been drunk out of, and awaited washing up. But Sir Bernard said Mrs Kempson had consumed a yellow substance as part of her last meal. Two possibilities were considered: egg and custard. Custard was considered the more likely. These days if one has custard one simply opens a tin, in those days it was a powder boiled in milk before adding to other ingredients, so it is possible (but not probable) that the saucepan Miss Williams saw was used for this purpose. When I make the distinction between possible and probable it is because of the *possibility* of Mrs Kempson consuming custard that she may have washed up the breakfast things on Saturday and this might have been her later Saturday or Sunday activities; or did she use a dirty saucepan? It is surprising Dr Dickson was unable to comment on when Mrs Kempson consumed custard. All in all though, it is *possible* Dr Dickson and Miss Williams were right and the time of death was on the Saturday morning, but *possible* leaves room for doubt.

Sir Bernard said the post-mortem examination would not allow him to say with certainty when death occurred but he did say that Dr Dickson's assessment was 'consistent' with his findings. 'Consistent' does not mean 'exactly the same', it means that Dr Dickson's theory could not be disproved; when something is not disproved it falls into the 'maybe' part of 'yes, no or maybe'.

'This enquiry was hampered in the early stages by local tradesmen and others who made statements ... that they saw Mrs Kempson about the neighbourhood after midday on the 1 August, but in view of evidence of medical and other witnesses their statements must be ruled out.' But what medical evidence? The medical evidence did not prove anything.

However, leaving the medical evidence aside, what did people claim they saw in the afternoon of 1 August? Mr William Lowe, a bricklayer, said that on the Saturday morning he saw Mrs Kempson at around 11.20 a.m.; he said she came from the direction of her house, went to a pillar box and posted a letter before he 'lost sight of her'. He denied he had spoken to newspaper reporters or anyone else. In court, counsel for the prosecution suggested that what he saw was actually on Friday and not Saturday. Mr Lowe, however, was sure it was the Saturday. He had seen her from a pub in the locality and the judge asked him if he went to this pub frequently, to which he replied he did (each day). So he may have mistaken one day for another. August is not usually a month noted for bricklayers to be out of work – January possibly, but not August – but it was not asked if he was off work at all that week, which would have made Saturday stick out in his mind.

Edgington's was a baker's shop that was almost opposite Mrs Kempson's house, and Mrs Sarah King said that as she was leaving the shop she passed Mrs Kempson who nodded and smiled. The time was around 11.30 a.m. She might have been mistaken but there is another witness to Mrs Kempson going to this baker's shop.

The assistant in the shop, Miss Evelyn Barrett, said she remembered Mrs Kempson came into the shop between 11.15 and 11.30 a.m. Mrs Kempson said she had just finished her housework. Miss Barrett quoted Mrs Kempson to say 'that she (Mrs Kempson) was going away tomorrow'. An issue was made about what Mrs Kempson bought each day, which was a small loaf. Sliding Miss Williams back under the microscope for a moment, when she returned to the house there was half a loaf of bread remaining, just as she left it. But that does not account for Mrs Kempson having her breakfast after Miss Williams had left the house, and the loaf she bought on the Saturday was half eaten on the Sunday morning. In his summary, Mr Justice Swift asked where the bread had gone – Sir Bernard found some of it in Mrs Kempson's stomach. So does this support Miss Williams' assertion that the breakfast table was as she left it? Are two things possible – firstly was this how Mrs Kempson habitually laid the table, so one day was just as the next; and, secondly, if Miss Williams saw the bread was as she had left it, then where did the bread come from in Mrs Kempson's stomach? So was it that Mrs Kempson (possibly with her 10.00 a.m. guest) finished the loaf Miss Williams saw, and then bought another – and was seen doing so by two witnesses – to eat (albeit partly) on the Sunday morning. DCI Horwell would say Mrs Kempson was too 'careful' with her money to buy bread she would not eat, but Monday's newspaper (which she would not read as she would be on holiday) was still delivered.

As Miss Barrett was giving her evidence she appeared to fall faint. She denied that a number of newspaper reporters had approached her, but admitted to speaking to one. So just assuming these two witnesses who support each other were right, then Mrs Kempson visited a shop after her 'death'.

Mr John Woodward was the assistant in a grocer's shop who said he served Mrs Kempson with butter 'between 12.00 and 1.00 p.m. on Saturday 1 August'. He could not remember the quantity but could remember it was the 'Countess' brand, which had only come in the day before. Counsel for the prosecution asked:

'Do you remember telling Ins Horwell that you might have made a mistake?'
'No, I do not remember saying that?'
'Will you swear you did not say it?'
'I didn't say it.'

Later counsel again tried to shake him in his evidence:

'I suggest to you that you sold Mrs Kempson half a pound of butter and that it was
    either on Thursday or Friday?'
'No. It was Saturday.'

The witness had spoken to newspaper reporters. His employer, to whom he was related, was William Woodward. He said Mrs Kempson had been in the shop after 12.00 on the Saturday and bought some butter. He added, 'The previous evening, Friday, 31 July, Mrs. Kempson had come into my shop and I served her with a pound of lump sugar and half a pound of chocolates.' Mr Woodward denied that he discussed the matter at 'great length' with newspaper reporters. Counsel for the defence objected to the prosecution going over the local paper, which was giving the reporter's view of events. Mr Justice Swift overruled the objection. Counsel for the prosecution read an extract from a report of the *Oxford Mail* of 6 August:

'"Mr. Woodward's contention was that Mrs. Kempson intended to take the butter
    away with her so that she could have it on holiday." Did you say that?'
'No.'
'Do you think that the reporter invented it?'

Mr Frederick Taylor had known Mrs Kempson for over twenty years and said he last saw her alive on Saturday 1 August between 12.30 and 12.40 p.m. He said he saw her leave her house and come out of the front garden – he said it looked as though she was going shopping. She apparently 'bowed' to Mr Taylor and he acknowledged it. Mr Taylor was a painter and decorator so it is likely Saturday would be different to the rest of the week when he was working. He said that when he saw Mrs Kempson he was going to catch a bus to go fishing.

The times Mr Taylor gives are 'consistent' with the times recorded by Mrs King and Miss Barrett in the baker's and both Mr John and Mr William Woodward in the grocer's. Mrs Kate Barson had known Mrs Kempson all of her life and said she saw her between 2.50 and 3.00 p.m. in St Clements Street on the afternoon of 1 August. She denied she may have mistaken Mrs Kempson for someone else, and she was with her husband, Mr Ernest Barson, who said he was 'quite close to her ... I should have bumped into her but my wife pulled me away'. However, Mrs Kempson did not speak to either Mr or Mrs Barson.

Mildred Green and Nellie Gregory also made statements to the effect they saw Mrs Kempson but there is no information available about when they saw her, or where. Neither gave evidence in court.

And finally, the eleventh witness who said she saw Mrs Kempson alive after mid-morning on 1 August was Mrs Florence Kirk, who said she saw Mrs Kempson in the late afternoon. At the trial, counsel for the prosecution suggested she had checked with her daughter regarding the date and time. Mrs Kirk said she did not do anything of the sort.

Whilst it is acknowledged that a brutal murderer was about town, it does make one wonder at the police's attitude towards some of the witnesses. A Mr Horne and Miss Reedes both made statements about the man who visited Mrs Kempson on the Saturday morning, but another witness saw this too. And, bearing in mind that despite what DCI Horwell said, the medical evidence did not support the assertion that the time of death was between 9.45 and 11.00 a.m. on that Saturday morning, then the police attitude to anyone who suggested otherwise appears a little lacking in decorum. I give an abridged quote from DCI Horwell's report:

> Another witness, Arthur Barrett, of Bath Street, which is not far from Mrs Kempson's house, states that at about 9.50 a.m., Saturday, he saw a man standing on the pavement a few yards from Mrs Kempson's house. The man appeared agitated and to be looking about. This went on for about 20 minutes and he thinks the man went into the Almshouses next door. The man was carrying a drab coloured raincoat, but the description does not quite tally with the description given by Miss Reedes and Mr Horn.

This might have been the man Miss Reedes saw; however, this is DCI Horwell's opinion: 'Mr Barrett is an old man with very poor sight and I am afraid he cannot be relied upon, and he cannot be described as intelligent.' This is perfectly alright and in keeping with good detective work, that is until the last gratuitous seven words, which are an assumption.

One is left wondering at times as to what was the most important thing to the police – a conviction, irrespective, or the detection of the actual criminal. Henry was an out-and-out crook, but there is no proof he was a murderer.

Part 15

It is possible that *some* of the people who said they saw Mrs Kempson after lunchtime on the Saturday were mistaken, but even so, eleven is a formidable number of people to discredit. Most of the attempts at this were made during the trial and clearly the jury believed evidence was gleaned from witnesses by the prosecution. But as I will discuss later, he only showed the *possibility* of them making a mistake, and one might be forgiven for thinking this was not enough, he had to *prove* they had made a mistake. One of the witnesses (the grocer) said Mrs Kempson had visited his shop on the Friday evening (31 July) and bought some sugar. This was argued to be in error, because Mrs

Kempson went shopping with a friend on Friday night, and then went to visit her brother. But it seems strange that collectively, and with the medical evidence (setting aside the recollections of Dr Dickson and Miss Williams), it was not accepted there was a reasonable doubt. So, albeit briefly, the Friday night's activities can be shown.

Mrs Kempson was friendly with a Mrs Ruth Steele on whom she called at around 5.30 p.m. on the Friday evening, and the two ladies went shopping. Mrs Kempson bought a new pair of shoes. It is unclear just how friendly the two ladies were or how long they had known each other. However, their shopping trip was not exhaustive and Mrs Steele got off the bus close to her home at around 7.00 p.m. Mrs Kempson was going on to her brother's house so she stayed on the bus. But it is not beyond the bounds of possibility that Mrs Kempson was back near to her own home within an hour or two. If she was, then as Mr Woodward's (the grocer) recollection suggests that she came into his shop and bought sugar, this may be correct as to the date, but with the timing could be way out. The point of this is that the prosecution at the trial convinced the jury that Mrs Kempson could not possibly have bought sugar in his shop on the Friday evening as she was out shopping with Mrs Steele and then visited her brother. Mrs Kempson's brother said he last saw her (which suggests that was the time of her leaving his house) at 8.30 p.m. on the Friday night. Mr Woodward had closed his shop and was at the point of leaving at 9.30 p.m. This would suggest he closed his shop at 9.00 p.m. but as he knew Mrs Kempson he might have let her have the sugar after he had closed – so is it possible she covered the distance from her brother's house about half way along Sandfield Road back to St Clements Street in half an hour or so? It is too far to walk, but if she was a frequent visitor to her brother, which she probably was, then it is possible she would know the bus times back towards the city centre and the journey time would be ten to fifteen minutes. Add five or even ten more minutes to let her get from her brother's house out onto the main Headington Road, and a good ten minutes for the bus to travel the distance. So, even with a generous margin, it gives her time to get back to Mr Woodward's shop, probably before it closed. The problem with this is Mr Woodward, who said Mrs Kempson came into his shop between 6.00 and 7.00 p.m. One has to ask though, is it possible Mrs Kempson went into the shop before her shopping trip?

But there is a part of Mrs Steele's story that does not sit comfortably. Mrs Kempson was deaf and, as DCI Horwell pointed out, she would leave her front door unlocked. Another witness, Miss Julia Life, described herself as a friend of Mrs Kempson and she described how she would open Mrs Kempson's front door and just go straight into her house. This is important, because when Miss Life called on 1 August she described how 'I tried the handle of the front door.' When Ruth Steele, the friend with whom Mrs Kempson had been shopping, brought the shoes Mrs Kempson had bought around to her house on the Saturday morning, she knocked at the door and rang the bell and even peeped through a small gap in the door; she then opened a window and threw the shoes into Mrs Kempson's front room. This seems odd because, as a friend, would she not know of Mrs Kempson's habit of leaving the door unlocked? Would she not simply open the door, or at any rate try it, and place the shoes just inside the door, or even go into the house – could she not have left the shoes in the porch for that matter? But instead she opened a window and threw the shoes in.

Miss Hilda Brown, who had known Mrs Kempson for some years and had always assisted her with the cleaning, said she habitually entered Mrs Kempson's by turning the handle of the door. As a rule, she arrived at the house just before 10.00 a.m. So a cleaner and a friend walked straight in, but a shopping companion did not even try and just threw the shoes in through an open window. This may have been perfectly normal, but it seems strange reciting the story now, and again a part of the story that tends to throw up more questions that beg for answers.

Her friend of many years and gardener Mr Charles James was expecting Mrs Kempson to call into his shop in the late afternoon of 1 August, which she had said she would do. In the event, she did not. Every Saturday, without fail, Mrs Kempson would go to the cemetery to tidy and maintain her husband's grave. However, it later transpired she did not do this on Saturday 1 August. This might have been because as she was going away for two weeks and she may have planned to leave it until the last possible moment on the Sunday to do this job. But, whatever the case, all this proves is that she did not do the job on the Saturday. If Mr James was expecting her at her usual time late in the afternoon – he said 'afternoon or evening' in his evidence – this weakens the theory that Mrs Kempson still had a breakfast on the Sunday, but it does not prove she was dead by 11.00 a.m., the latest that Henry could have killed her. So her not tending the grave on the Saturday could point to her death on the Saturday, but later than the police and the prosecution were willing to accede to.

After the post-mortem, Sir Bernard said:

> I cannot fix the time of death at all accurately from the post-mortem change at the time when I examined the body, She must have been dead for at least 24 hours and the condition of the body is consistent with her having been dead since the previous Saturday morning (1 August) but not for much longer or I should have expected to find putrefactive changes commencing. The death occurred not more than about two hours after the last meal.

If Mrs Kempson bought bread on the Saturday then it is possible the meal found in her stomach was a slice or two of bread and butter she might have had at lunchtime. He also found a 'yellow substance', which was thought to be custard. If Mrs Kempson was going away and had a bit of spare milk then she might have made custard.

So we have a bit of a mystery. Another mystery was the weapon: chisel or screwdriver? The hammer (which was not the murder weapon) was found in the luggage Henry left at the Greyhound Hotel in Aylesbury. The police said he disposed of the screwdriver or chisel. Why not dispose of both tools? Likewise, a pathologist could tell by the state of the skin if a 'blunt' implement had been used to make the wound in Mrs Kempson's throat, but Sir Bernard said a 'sharp cutting tool'.

At this point, I need to reintroduce the chisel dilemma. In a report by Sir Bernard, dated 25 August, he discusses a 'knife': 'There would have been blood on the knife used for stabbing.' This can only refer to the wound in Mrs Kempson's neck, which was variously suggested to have been caused by the chisel or a screwdriver. A pathologist would be able to ascertain what the weapon was, its shape and degree of sharpness. When DCI Horwell had taken statements from the manager at Fulkes' ironmonger's, there was some discussion about the chisel and some suggestion as to what chisel was sold, with no direct evidence that it had been sold to Henry. As it had been in a batch of three (of which one remained), DCI Horwell took the third chisel for Sir Bernard to examine. But Sir Bernard does not connect the (sample) chisel with the wound in Mrs Kempson's neck at all, and is at pains to point out he cannot connect either the hammer or the chisel to the wounds found on Mrs Kempson.

The judge was dismissive of the pathological findings but the prosecution did not seek the opinion of another pathologist. It might have been a bit embarrassing if they did because Sir Bernard was engaged by the Home Office, or in short, he was on *their* side.

Indirectly, what this part suggests is that evidence was withheld from the jury as to the timings on the Friday night after Mrs Kempson had left her brother's house; that the screwdriver/chisel had mysteriously disappeared and the pathologist said the hammer they did find – and the chisel they did not find – were not the weapons used. Were the jury adequately prepared to judge properly and fairly?

Part 16

It was thought that after battering Mrs Kempson into eternity, Henry ransacked the house, stealing as he went. But the pounding on the front door and ringing of the bell by Mrs Steele unnerved him. So it was not in the prosecution's interest for Mrs Steele to try the door. But was it known that the probability was that Mrs Kempson did not open her front door because she was deaf and therefore did not hear it?

This is what Mr Justice Swift said in his summing up:

> At 11.00 a.m., Mrs Steele knocked at the door and rang the bell. Receiving no reply she tossed the shoes inside the front window on to a settee and they were found by the police in the same position. Is it not clear that she was dead at the time Mrs. Steele called?

No, it is not clear. If the judge did not know Mrs Kempson was deaf then one has to ask the same of the jury? Could they have judged the facts in this case with this fact of Mrs Kempson's deafness hidden from them? Moreover, it is possible that Mrs Kempson did not find the shoes as she had no reason for going into that room that morning. As she was going away and Miss Williams had already gone, is it possible she just simply did not enter this room that morning or early afternoon? 'Is it not clear...?' No, my Lord – what is clear is that Mrs Kempson may not have heard Mrs Steele and she might not have had reason to go into that room for the entire day, but might well have still been alive.

So did Mrs Steele, with her knocking on the door and ringing the bell, actually frighten Henry and prompt his quick exit? This has little to support it, and as he had spent time in prison and housebreaking was not new to him, he may have had a callous disregard or contempt for Mrs Steele (and everybody else for that matter) – but a 'fear' is only a possibility. In summing up the evidence, the judge should do just that – sum up – not ask the jury about what is or is not clear, especially as it is open to interpretation, and when he said 'Is it not clear...?' He is prompting the jury's thinking.

DCI Horwell went to a lot of trouble himself to prove Henry was the killer and said:

> In my endeavour to reconstruct the crime, I have formed the opinion that the dustbin, having been placed in the hall by Mrs Kempson on the morning of 1 August, gave the murderer the opportunity to stun her from behind.

He bases this assertion on the fact there was no room at the front door for Mrs Kempson to open the door fully and invite her guest in, therefore she walked ahead of him down the hall and into the back parlour where he struck her with the hammer. The murder may well have happened in this way, but it only shifts emphasis away from Henry and to the killer's possible method so does not actually establish anything. She was struck from behind, probably with a hammer, and she fell to the floor where she was struck on two further occasions before she was stabbed with a sharp cutting tool in the neck. The judge said this wound could have equally been caused by a screwdriver or a chisel, but this cannot be supported by the evidence presented in court: screwdrivers are not sharp cutting tools, and Sir Bernard actually referred to a 'knife'.

Just to digress for a moment to further consider the search for the chisel, the Sussex Police searched the flat Henry had rented in Brighton, but found neither a chisel nor a screwdriver. Henry said he put the tools in his luggage at the hotel in Aylesbury – luggage that was searched and later removed. So one can identify a scenario whereby Henry puts the screwdriver in his luggage and then a policeman does not find it; but all this is Henry *saying* he put the screwdriver in the luggage and the policeman *saying* he did not find it. The fact is that a screwdriver is not a sharp cutting instrument and a chisel is (one is inclined to remember Percival Andrews' statement, which said he did *not* see it). It leaves the question of what happened to the screwdriver or chisel. If the police knew – and they did – Sir Bernard thought the hammer found in Henry's possession and the (sample) chisel borrowed from Fulkes' 'failed to correspond' with the injuries to Mrs Kempson's head, then it would not help their case. It is possible to make a screwdriver disappear, but it is not possible to change a screwdriver into a chisel.

As for motive, Henry certainly had financial difficulties which a good haul from a good theft would have helped. He would know Mrs Kempson was deaf so burgling the house under the cover of darkness would have perhaps been more profitable than entering the house with a hammer and screwdriver/chisel flailing everywhere. He needed a good bit of money though. He owed £96 to Yarnstrong's and a further £25 to the car hire firm, which would be equivalent to about £5,500 by 2010, so it might be as well for him to disappear for a while. Moving from Oxford circuitously to Brighton under an assumed name may have helped but he had other plans. The Sussex Police searched his flat in Brighton and found 'an envelop [*sic*] addressed to Mr F Harvey and one addressed to Cook's Shipping Office, Brighton, and containing an *application form for a position of steward on a ship* [Author's italics]'.

DCI Horwell's ideas were aired in court but he was examined and cross-examined at length. The police were trying to make the pieces fit a theory that they did not fit. The police investigation was concluded and DCI Horwell commented, 'This case against Seymour cannot be said to be strong, but it contains a chain of small links of very suspicious incidents and circumstantial evidence.'

There were certainly some suspicious incidents where Henry could not be seen to act as any other person would act, and parts of his story, on a continuum from fact to fiction, would be difficult to place. But this only demonstrates that he is a vague, odd and far-from-honest character. The theft of his money whilst he was bathing sounds as though it came out of a semi-illiterate crime thriller and his walk to Revd Green's suggests he is hiding something he does not really need to hide.

But it is difficult to see a 'chain' of events in this case which would support the assertion of circumstantial evidence. So it would help now to briefly consider the trial and the summing up to think further about the weak points of the case.

Part 17

The trial opened at Oxford Assize Court on Tuesday 20 October and ran for five days. Mr Justice Rigby Swift presided. Mr St John Micklethwait KC led for the prosecution and Mr William Earengey KC appeared for the defence.

Mr Micklethwait opened the case for the Crown; he described the history of the murder and introduced Henry Daniel Seymour as the man whose guilt or innocence was for scrutiny. He had no alibi for the material times, he had the motive and he had the opportunity. But lying at the core of the case were the two questions:

　　1. At what time was Mrs Kempson attacked and murdered?
　　2. What evidence was there that Henry actually killed her?

Mr Micklethwait suggested that a hammer and a sharp wood chisel were used to kill Mrs Kempson. With the hammer came the prosecution's first problem because Sir Bernard for the Home Office was a leading prosecution witness who did not think the hammer the prosecution presented was the murder weapon. Nor was there the remotest possibility that the neck wound was inflicted by a wood chisel. Mr Micklethwait, however, suggested the size difference between the striking surface of the hammer and the wound was, in the case of the first blow, made up for by the bun of hair on the back of the victim's head and thereafter Henry covered the hammer with some fabric that gave a wound slightly larger than the striking surface. It seems a bit farfetched for a killer to change the configuration of the weapon after blow number one, but before the second and third blows. But that is what the prosecution contended and therefore that is what the jury should consider.

　　Henry made no secret of the fact he bought some tools on the day preceding the murder, but there was never any proof he had a chisel in his possession. But Mrs Andrews said she saw a chisel wrapped in a parcel:

> I did not undo the parcels. The paper was torn about two inches from the top of the chisel ... the blade end. I saw about two inches of the blade end. I think I should be able to recognise a similar instrument. The part of the instrument I saw was about three-quarters of an inch in width. The paper wrapping on the hammer was broken at the top – the head end.

And, according to DCI Horwell, Percival Andrews, her son, said:

> Mrs Andrews' son showed Seymour where he could hang his hat and raincoat in the hall and when Seymour took his raincoat off he was seen to pull from one of the pockets a new hammer and a new chisel, wrapped separately in brown paper which was torn. He put the tools on the floor of the hall. Young Andrews noticed a label on the handle of the hammer and that the chisel was about ¾ inch in width. He saw the blade but not the handle.

In court, the evidence of Percival Andrews was carefully controlled lest he let the jury know what he actually saw (or did not see); this is what he said in his deposition:

(Henry) took out of a pocket of the raincoat two packages one of which contained a hammer of which I saw part of the head ... The other parcel was well wrapped up and I did not see what was in it. He put the parcels down by the hall stand and said he would leave them there until morning.

The two issues here were the false claim by the police of what Percival Andrews saw, and that his evidence cast doubt on what his mother said she saw. So if the doctrine of reasonable doubt is (or was) alive and well, then there has to be reasonable doubt that Henry had a chisel with him. He did purchase a hammer and a screwdriver, but when the staff of the hardware shop gave evidence there was no proof he lied and that one of the tools was a chisel.

Sir Bernard also said in his evidence that Mrs Kempson had a yellowish substance in her stomach which was considered to be custard. This negates the evidence of Miss Williams, and also Dr Dickson who examined Mrs Kempson's body where it was found. And Miss Williams could remember the exact layout of the breakfast things five or so days later – a remarkable feat of memory, unless a Sunday morning breakfast spread was similar to Saturdays, and similar to Fridays. Mr Earengey for the defence closely cross-examined Sir Bernard as to the time death took place:

'Was there anything to suggest, that the crime was not committed before Saturday evening?'
'No, as far as my examina¬tion went, there was nothing that would help me to fix it as near as that.'

Recalled and cross-examined by Mr Earengey, Dr Dickson said he came to the conclusion that death took place between 10.00 a.m. and 12.00 noon on 1 August, because a meal had been taken in the kitchen, and nothing had been washed up and there was no preparation for a midday meal.

Mr Earengey: 'I want to know what medical reasons you have got?'
Answer: 'None...'

That left the evidence of Mrs Steele who came to the house at around 11.00 a.m. to drop off the shoes Mrs Kempson had purchased. She rang the bell and knocked on the door, but got no answer. Mr Justice Swift said, 'is it not clear she was dead?' Mrs Kempson was deaf so the possibility was she did not hear so this did not prove that she was dead at 11.00 a.m. Mr Justice Swift also said it was odd Mrs Kempson did not examine or look at the shoes – that assumes she knew they were there, it is possible if she was going away on holiday she had tidied and closed off the front parlour. And she would not have heard the window opening and the shoes thrown in – and I have still some difficulty in the fact that, as a friend, Mrs Steele did not try the front door as Mrs Kempson's other friends said they usually did.

The fact that Henry had moved from Oxford circuitously to Brighton, owing money here and there (in considerable sums), and had acted as an all-round suspicious character (which he was) did not help his defence at all.

But this was the sum of the prosecution's case.

For the defence, Mr Earengey said that the facts as presented by the prosecution asserted that the murder took place on the Saturday morning. Miss Williams left at 9.20 a.m. and then Mrs Kempson prepared and ate her breakfast. This would take the clock round to perhaps 9.50 a.m. Mr Earengey concluded that if Sir Bernard was right about the time of death being something like an hour to an hour and a half after her last meal then this would bring the time round to, he said, twenty minutes past eleven before the first blow was struck:

> It was quite clear from the evidence, of the Crown that at three minutes past 11 the prisoner was seen in no hurry one mile and 520 yards away from the place where the murder was committed. It must have taken him about 20 minutes to walk that distance.
>
> If these times were all reckoned up it was obvious that the prisoner had no time to commit the offence and to have got up to where he was seen. That being so, the case for the prosecution was clearly inconsistent. The times were the prosecution's …

But the argument is weak. Pathologists can only give an approximation of how long after a meal a person has died; if they have the exact time the meal was taken, which they did not, then it helps, but it is still not exact.

There was another problem for Mr Earengey revolving around Sir Bernard. He was the pathologist who had 'rescued' the branch of medicine and reaffirmed its professional base, and by 1931 he was fifty-four and would have been at the height of his professional skills. But this brought consternation from lawyers – he was labelled as arrogant and his delivery of evidence in court was confident to the point of irritation. But he had prejudices which may have clouded his professional judgement. He shied away from passing on his skills to junior members of the profession and did not get along with his peers. But, on the other hand, he was a witness for the prosecution and his delivery of evidence in this particular case may have been quite objective: he could not pinpoint the time of death and said so. Even today the state of the digestion can only give a rough guide to the time of death and that still relies on a number of factors that were not known in Mrs Kempson's case. He also stated that the hammer found in Henry's possession did not cause the wounds on Mrs Kempson's head. Both the police and the prosecution (I can discuss what the judge said a little later) said he did not allow for the bun of hair on the back of her head to help create a larger wound than the striking face of the hammer would give. Possibly this is true, but there were two other wounds on her head. So the possibility is raised that Henry placed some kind of material over the striking face of the hammer and this gave the impression that it was larger. This assumes a lot more skill and knowledge than the average killer may have.

By this time in his career Sir Bernard had rankled many lawyers, and there were three here – the prosecution, the defence and the judge. His evidence was for the Crown but was far more supportive of the defence – so this would irritate the prosecution, but they were stuck with him because the Home Office directed he would conduct such post-mortem examinations. Once the defence knew what he was going to say they need not and did not call in their own expert, and the judge made his feelings very clear in his summing up. To top it all, the police said Sir Bernard made some quite elementary mistakes in his evidence, which was dubious. So in among this mayhem of a battered lady and an utter crook in the dock was a strong odour of a medico-legal political undercurrent.

Mr Earengey said in the conclusion of his opening speech:

> In my submission, it is clearly impossible for my client to have been concerned in this. I am going to call witnesses to say that they saw Mrs. Kempson alive between 11 and 12 o'clock that morning posting a letter, about 12 o'clock in a shop buying some butter, and between 12 and one o'clock buying a loaf of bread. And in the afternoon you will have two people who saw her.

But the witnesses the defence called were not as convincing as hoped, and were susceptible to the prosecution's tactics to generally undermine them by quoting from what they were supposed to have said to the press. Mr Earengey for the defence objected to this prosecution 'evidence'. The judge advised Mr Micklethwait for the prosecution that he should refrain from this – but was the damage this tactic may have caused already done? This type of tactic by the prosecution is all very well to win the case, but even though it might impress the jury, does it actually serve justice? And does it leave the real killer on the loose?

Henry gave evidence, but as was his personality it was vague and at times contradictory. He was easy prey, a crook, a con-man and a thief, and it is very easy to prejudice a jury. The criminal law is there to check the wrongdoing of the wrongdoer, but to get a murder conviction and a death penalty to stop some thieving is to show life through the eye of a walnut, as a sledgehammer hurtles towards it.

Saturday – the fifth day of the trial – was occupied by the counsels' closing speeches and the judge's summing up. Mrs Steele was recalled to give evidence that Mrs Kempson was in her company between 5.30 and 7 p.m. on the Friday evening (31 July). As far as she knew, Mrs Kempson did not call at Woodward's shop – the grocer's. Replying to Mr Earengey, Mrs Steele said that she left Mrs Kempson on the bus going to Headington. Mr Robert Reynolds, Mrs Kempson's brother, was also recalled: 'I last saw my sister at around 8.30 pm on the 31 July when she called at my home.'

In his deposition, Mr Woodward, the grocer, said Mrs Kempson called between 6.00 and 7.00 p.m. on the Friday night and again on the Saturday. But she could not have called at that time as she was elsewhere.

Little could be done by the defence to account for the fact Henry had taken the label off the hammer, which suggested he would not want the hammer traced, and there was the general assumption that this was so he could batter Mrs Kempson with it. But would a housebreaker also try to disguise his tools?

Part 18

After all the speeches and the evidence came the judge's summing up. These are the central points, but with some discussion:

Mrs Annie Louisa Kempson was murdered.

Henry Daniel Seymour was arrested at Brighton, brought to Oxford, cautioned and charged.

The judge said, 'You must decide this case on the evidence given.'

All through the trial Mr Justice Rigby seems to have been unaware of Mrs Kempson's deafness, yet DCI Horwell mentions it in his report and therefore it is not an idle assumption that Mr Micklethwait for the prosecution also knew it.

The judge went on, 'If this woman was murdered who did the murder?' Involved in that question is, if she was murdered, then when?

'Before you return a verdict against the prisoner you must he satisfied that she was murdered between 9.30 and 11 o'clock on 1 August.' This was because Henry did not have a satisfactory alibi for these times.

'Mrs. Steele ... agreed she would take (the shoes) round and receive some beans and flowers, at 11.00 a.m. At 11.00 a.m., Mrs Steele knocked the door and rang the bell. Is it not clear that she was dead at the time Mrs. Steele called?' This tends to confirm that the judge did not know she was deaf and there was the possibility (or probability) Mrs Kempson did not hear Mrs Steele. As a consequence, he is giving an opinion, which cannot be supported by the facts as far as they are known.

'There is the evidence of Mr. James', which doesn't really take us anywhere apart from the fact that Mrs Kempson was not sticking to her usual routine for a Saturday in attending her husband's grave.

'Can there be any doubt that she was dead at 11 o'clock on that Saturday morning.' Yes, there can be doubt, and reasonable doubt too. The medical examinations did not pinpoint her time of death and witnesses claim to have seen her after 11.00 a.m. Even though some can be demonstrated to have been mistaken, some were not examined in court and their depositions seem sound.

There was definitely a visitor to Mrs Kempson's house and he was seen by two witnesses: Miss Reedes and Mr Horn. Both said they could recognise the man again (although they only saw him from the back!) and DCI Horwell wanted an identification parade but none is recorded.

The body was found on Monday evening. The defence say that she ... died on the Sunday. Sir Bernard Spilsbury, said, 'I could not tell within twenty four or thirty six hours when this death took place. But I can say death took place within twelve hours of eating tomatoes and between one and two hours after she had had something to eat consisting bread and butter and custard.'

'Doctor Dixon [*sic*] formed the opinion that she died on Saturday morning and gives reasons, the port-mortem and the condition of the house and the woman.' No medical reason as to time of death and the 'evidence' about the state of the kitchen is only guesswork. To reinforce Dr Dickson's 'opinion', which cannot be supported by the facts, the judge may be misdirecting the jury.

The medics could not help. As for a meal on the Saturday night, Miss Williams said nearly a week later that the remains of the tomatoes Mrs Kempson may have eaten on the Friday night were still in evidence. Was it possible Mrs Kempson had washed up after Miss Williams had gone, and the tomatoes were from after this, and the cups and saucers were from later, and the pan for boiling milk for custard, again, later? And her guest on Saturday morning – is it possible she had a cup of tea with him, hence two cups and saucers?

'Where was the loaf which she purchased on the Saturday. If she bought a pound of butter on Saturday where is it?' These are interesting questions, and they cannot be reconciled with the known facts. But if the loaf Miss Williams said was left in the same place, then where did the bread come from that Sir Bernard said he found in Mrs Kempson's stomach?

'Mr Taylor, said he saw Mrs. Kempson come out of her house at 12.30 p.m. If the lady had been shopping that morning why would she go out again?' The answer to that is to post a letter, and perhaps she was guilty of that dreadful human failing of forgetting the letter earlier. There may be a multitude of reasons why she should go out again. The judge went on:

Mrs. Kirk says that she saw Mrs Kempson in Cornmarket on Saturday afternoon, but Mrs Kempson had been shopping the day previous when she had purchased new shoes. It is said she spent the whole of that Saturday going in and out shopping, posting a letter etc., and that she left the new shoes on the Chesterfield.

No doubt *Mrs* Justice Swift was organised. If Mrs Kempson was not then he was not going to understand. And Mrs Kempson might not have known her shoes were on the sofa!

'A main point is whether she had done her household duties or not is what the police found on visiting Miss Williams room.' This cannot be accounted for except her visitor may have distracted her. And what is there to prove someone did not call later and kill her – she had simply put this job off as Miss Williams was away.

'Mr Lowe went to get some bones for his dog and tells us that went to the Coach and Horses for a drink ... he saw Mrs Kempson put something in the letter box ... his regular routine except for the bones for his dog. He may have seen Mrs. K. on the Tuesday, Wednesday, Thursday or Friday.' Mr Lowe said he had bones for his dog which he always got on a Saturday.

'If he saw a letter posted on Saturday, is it conceivable that somebody would have come forward to say that they received it?' Possibly, but it might have been a business letter and the person receiving it may not have been aware of its significance.

'Mr Taylor, was going fishing, his usual occupation for a Saturday morning. It is the easiest thing in the world, in the hubbub and excitement when this thing occurred for the incident which he thought occurred on Saturday, 1 August occurred on another day.' Possibly, but this is an opinion which goes against the known facts.

'Mr. and Mrs. Barson say they saw Mrs. K. at about 3 o'clock. The prosecution say that if she was out at 3.00 pm, that afternoon she did not go to her husband's grave. Mrs Barson said she had known Mrs K. all her life and Mr Barson said he had known Mrs. K. for some time. Both say that Mrs. K. did not recognise them.' So there may have been a reason Mrs Kempson did not seem to notice them.

'Was she murdered at 10 o'clock or directly after it by the man who Horn saw go into house. There is only one person who knows what happened in that house. He was a man 5ft 4in in height, in a dark suit, no hat. The door was opened and he went in. Mrs Kempson knew the prisoner. Prisoner had been in the habit of going to her house.' There is no evidence to support this. Henry called and followed up most people who bought one of his vacuum cleaners. There is no proof it was Henry who went to her house that morning. And it was thought Henry had knocked at about ten minutes to ten but received no answer, so returned. At ten minutes to ten it was Miss Reedes who saw him, but ten minutes later he had gained about four inches in height and had lost his cap.

Mr Justice Swift continued, 'He left Oxford under a cloud.' Without doubt. The money he embezzled from Yarnstrong's together with the money he owed the car hire firm has an equivalent value today of about £5,500.

'He told Mrs Andrews his money was stolen, that he had no money, and wanted to go to Aylesbury or Thame. She lent him 4/6d and he then sprinted or ran in the direction of Headington. He says he caught a bus, the prosecution say he got to Fulkes' shop and purchased a hammer and chisel. A man went in the shop, according to Mr Fulkes, and bought a hammer and chisel. The prosecution suggest that the man who bought these articles was the prisoner.'

There is no proof of any of this; in fact, Mrs Andrews' son neutralises her evidence. Henry freely admitted he had bought a hammer and a screwdriver. Mr Justice Swift said 'a screwdriver might have caused the injuries.'

No matter what the legal establishment thought of Sir Bernard Spilsbury he could tell the difference between a wound made by a sharp cutting instrument and a blunt instrument. Mr Justice Swift is not questioning the evidence and presenting it for deliberation; he is questioning its authenticity. It is perfectly acceptable for counsel to question authenticity usually by cross-examination or possibly calling another 'expert' witness. But they did not.

'Where was he at 3 minutes to 10. A man in blue suit, carrying a light coat, entered Mrs. Kempson's house. He was somewhere that morning between Mrs. Andrews' house which is about 12 minutes walk from Mrs. Kempson's house. He said he went to the Revd. Green's house. What for? He had nothing to collect, nothing to sell.' A very good point.

'The prosecution say "What was he doing between 9.30 when he left Mrs. Andrews' house until 11 o'clock when Mrs. Collins saw him?" The prosecution say that a man, at 4 minutes to 10, was at the door of Mrs Kempson's house, entered and murdered Mrs K."' They might say that, but the evidence they give is only suspicious and is not backed up by eyewitnesses or forensic evidence.

'No screwdriver was found or a chisel. Whoever obliterated those marks did it purposely and intending to destroy the identity of the hammer.' But for what reason: to evade capture for murder, or to capture for other crimes?

'Has the evidence convinced you that the man who went into that house was the prisoner, and, having been convinced, was the prisoner ...' What 'Evidence'? It could not be proved when Mrs Kempson died. No witness positively identified Henry – he was known in the area. There was nothing more than a suggestion Henry was on her doorstep at four minutes to ten. There was no proof he had a chisel. There was no proof the hammer he owned caused the injuries, in fact Sir Bernard said it did not.

With nothing more than suspicion of his guilt, but with their heads full of facts as to Henry's total lack of honesty, the jury retired. Forty minutes later, they declared him guilty.

Henry appealed. Mr Earengey commented (as above) on Mr Justice Swift's summing up in that 'in spite of the judge having formed his opinion it was his duty to put the case for the defence fairly'.

In reply, Lord Hewart said, 'I have read every word of his summing up and I do not observe anywhere in it an expression of the judge's opinion'.

Mrs Steele's evidence was that at 11.00 a.m. she knocked the knocker and rang the bell. Mr Justice Swift: 'Is it not clear that she was dead at the time Mrs. Steele called?' If that is not an opinion, then what is it? And in the event, it is a dubious opinion.

In relation to the 'sharp cutting tool' Sir Bernard Spilsbury said made the cut in Mrs Kempson's throat, Mr Justice Swift said, 'A screwdriver might well have caused the injuries'. If that is not an opinion, and one which was in conflict to the Home Office pathologist, then one can only guess at what Lord Hewart's definition of an opinion is.

Henry's appeal was dismissed.

He was hanged on 10 December 1931.

There was no evidence that Henry committed the crime, or when. Without any clear evidence of when Mrs Kempson was murdered, without positively identified weapons, and without any forensic or eyewitness evidence, one is left with the feeling that the real issues were Henry's dishonesty and his lack of alibi for one and a half hours for one morning in August 1931. It was this that ensured his *acquittal was denied*, so with the absence of what a conviction relies on, the murder of Mrs Annie Louisa Kempson on 1 August 1931 is an unsolved murder.

Sadly Mrs Kempson's house, Boundary House, is no more. This picture was taken from the junction opposite of St Clements Street and Cave Street (formerly George Street) where Mr Horn saw Mrs Kempson's visitor enter her house at 10.00 a.m.